D1142205

250
DAYS

250
DAYS

Cantona's Kung Fu and
the making of Manchester United

DANIEL STOREY

HarperCollins*Publishers*

HarperCollins*Publishers*
1 London Bridge Street
London SE1 9GF

www.harpercollins.co.uk

1 3 5 7 9 10 8 6 4 2

© Daniel Storey 2019

Daniel Storey asserts the moral right to be
identified as the author of this work

A catalogue record of this book is
available from the British Library

ISBN 978-0-00-832049-2

Printed and bound in Great Britain
by CPI Group (UK) Ltd, Croydon, CR0 4YY

MIX
Paper from
responsible sources
FSC
www.fsc.org FSC C007454

This book is produced from independently certified FSC paper
to ensure responsible forest management.

For more information visit: www.harpercollins.co.uk/green

CONTENTS

PRELUDE

'Are you big enough for me?'

Eric Cantona was not the first foreign footballer in England, but he might well have been the most influential. No single player better represents English football's rapid transformation from the working-class, kick-and-rush game of Division One – a sport that had largely remained the same for half a century – to the glamour and exoticism of the current Premier League.

Before the mid-1990s foreign players were a luxury item, mysterious circus animals tasked with performing for our entertainment. At that time, 'foreign' had a pejorative connotation: fancy, flash, weak-willed. Foreign imports could temporarily call England home, but it would never be their natural habitat. They would hate our weather, hate our food, hate the physicality of the game that we invented and then gave to the world. And they would soon leave for whence they had come.

That was odd, given the success of some memorable foreign imports in the late 1970s and early 1980s. Ossie Ardiles and Ricky Villa at Tottenham, Arnold Mühren and Frans Thijssen at Ipswich, Johnny Metgod at Nottingham Forest; all became fan favourites due to their natural talent and willingness to embrace the culture of their clubs. But their success did not provoke an immediate wave of immigration.

The first weekend of the inaugural Premier League in August 1992 demonstrated English football's insular nature. The 22 clubs handed appearances to only 13 non-British players. Four of those were goalkeepers and another four (John Jensen, Michel Vonk, Gunnar Halle and Roland Nilsson) were defensively minded players.

A high percentage of foreign players in the Premier League's early years were from northern European countries – Denmark, Sweden, Norway, the Netherlands. They were preferred not only on account of their assumed comfort in dealing with the British climate, but also because they came from countries where English football was already a staple. One of the first questions asked by a club owner or manager when signing a foreign player was 'Can he fit into the English game?'

'Having supported and followed English football all my life, like every other Norwegian, it was a dream to play in England,' former Swindon, Middlesbrough, Sheffield United and Bradford striker Jan Åge Fjørtoft says. 'We had grown up with *Match of the Day* every Saturday night, you see.'

Of the others, Andrei Kanchelskis and Anders Limpar were two who had skill as their primary characteristic, but the pair started only 26 league games between them for Manchester United and Arsenal in 1992/93. Ronny Rosenthal was a workmanlike Israeli striker for Liverpool who had become the most expensive non-British player to join an English club in

1990. Polish winger Robert Warzycha was the first player from mainland Europe to score a Premier League goal – for Everton – but managed only 18 starts in the competition before being sold to Hungarian side Pécsi MFC.

The Premier League was therefore desperate for a poster boy. Clubs had the means to pay higher wages thanks to a broadcasting deal with Sky Sports worth an initial £304 million. Many of the top-flight stadia had been improved following the recommendations of the Taylor Report. The stage had changed; the actors had not. In late 1992 the Premier League was nothing more than the old First Division rolled in glitter and studded with rhinestones.

Enter Eric Cantona and Manchester United. In November 1992, in strolled a Marseillais enigma whose confidence was only matched by the size of his reputation. With Leeds United keen to get rid of their tempestuous Gallic star, Alex Ferguson believed he had found the player around whom he could build the first age of his dynasty.

'If ever there was one player, anywhere in the world, that was made for Manchester United, it was Cantona,' as Ferguson would subsequently say. 'He swaggered in, stuck his chest out, raised his head and surveyed everything as though he were asking: "I'm Cantona. How big are you? Are you big enough for me?"'

More than any other player, it was Cantona who unlocked the door for the Premier League's foreign revolution. He proved that the skill European and South American players stereotypically possessed need not exclude the passion and will to win of the old English First Division. Just as Glenn Hoddle and Terry Butcher – two fixtures of the England national team in the 1980s – were as disparate in style as it is possible to conceive, so too could foreign players come from any part of the footballing spectrum. If that now sounds like an unnecessary truism, it was far from obvious in 1992.

But Cantona became more than a trailblazer; he was a cultural and sporting icon. No single player was more responsible for the boom in replica shirt sales and merchandising (official or otherwise), while the ubiquity of Cantona's face thanks to a sponsorship deal with Nike was new ground for English football. In a thousand playgrounds across the country, collars on school-uniform shirts were turned up as children mimicked the hallmark of their hero. For a few years every kid was Eric Cantona. If those children have now turned 30, many still harbour the same adoration.

Cantona's personality could never have been so influential without talent. He scored 82 times in 185 games for Manchester United, but it was his style of play that was so unusual. Before the Premier League era there was very little tactical fluidity in English football. Defenders defended and attackers attacked, and players typically stayed in formation.

Cantona preferred a different method. He started as a nominal strike partner – usually to Mark Hughes or Andy Cole – but dropped deep in between the lines of defence and midfield, dragging immobile central defenders out of their position and comfort zone. Cantona's technical expertise allowed him to link play effectively, and he became as renowned for his chance-creation as his finishing. Cantona is credited with 56 assists in 156 Premier League games. The only other strikers of his era to register more – Cole, Alan Shearer and Teddy Sheringham – all played at least 250 more matches.

Conversely, Cantona's talent could never have been so influential without personality. Cantona was a leader of Manchester United not just because of his talent, but through sheer strength of character. As Roy Keane so eloquently put it: 'Collar up, back straight, chest stuck out, he glided into the arena as if he owned the f***ing place. Any arena, but nowhere more effectively than Old Trafford. This was his stage. He loved it, the crowd loved him.'

Cantona's unwavering self-belief – it bordered on swaggering arrogance – was not a natural trait, but a deliberate tool of his success. 'I've said in the past that I could play single-handedly against eleven players and win,' he wrote in *Cantona on Cantona*. 'Give me a bicycle and I believe I can beat Chris Boardman's one-hour record.' In Cantona's psyche there was no room for doubt. Doubt is what leads to fear, and if fear cannot be controlled it eventually defeats you.

The Cantona effect at Manchester United became extraordinarily influential, but he was doubted when he joined. In hindsight, Leeds and their manager Howard Wilkinson are mocked for letting Cantona go, but they made a profit on the transfer fee they had paid to Nîmes less than 12 months earlier and had endured a rocky relationship with the Frenchman. Cantona failed to click with striker Lee Chapman, and later revealed his unhappiness at Elland Road. Wilkinson did the same: 'Eric is not prepared to abide by the rules and conditions which operate for everybody else here.'

'I had a bad relationship with the manager, Wilkinson,' Cantona told *FourFourTwo* in 2008. 'We didn't have the same views on football. I am more like a Manchester footballer. At Leeds, football was played the old way – I think you say kick then rush. If I don't feel the environment is good, I don't want to be there.' Cantona is right to some extent, but underplays his own role in United's 'new way'.

Senior Manchester United players Gary Pallister, Steve Bruce and Bryan Robson all raised significant concerns among each other and to the club about Cantona's reputation for upsetting team morale, but Lee Sharpe was the most candid. 'This bloke's a total nutter, what are we doing?' he is quoted as saying. The national media were hardly warm in their congratulations to Ferguson for his signing.

But Ferguson realised that his club needed a shot in the arm. They had finished second to Leeds the previous season, but sat eighth in the table with summer signing Dion Dublin out injured. Ferguson's team had won two of their previous 13 matches, and there were lingering doubts over the Scotsman's job security. United had not won the league title for 25 years.

Ferguson spoke to then-France national team manager Gérard Houllier for advice on Cantona, but also leant on Michel Platini and journalist Erik Bielderman for their input. The conclusion from all three was that Cantona needed a father figure, while Ferguson needed a new leader. Both men fitted the other's need perfectly. Cantona only had problems with authority when he did not respect it.

His impact was instantaneous. Manchester United won eight and drew two of his first ten league games, and the split across the whole of 1992/93 is striking: 1.5 points per league game before his arrival and 2.3 points per league game afterwards; 1.06 goals per league game before his arrival and 1.92 goals per league game afterwards. From being eighth in the league and nine points from the top, United finished the season as league champions, with a ten-point cushion to second place.

Alongside the results, Cantona changed the mood too. By New Year's Day 1993 Ferguson was publicly enthusing about Cantona's effect on every element of Manchester United. 'More than at any time since I was playing, the club is alive,' he said. 'It's as if the good old days are back and the major factor, as far as I'm concerned, is the Frenchman.'

Manchester United's former greats lined up to pour on praise. 'I can't think of anyone who I would rather wear my crown,' said Denis Law. George Best was even more effusive: 'I would pay to watch Cantona play. There are not many players over the years I would say that about. He is a genius.' Old Trafford had its new king.

But the appeal of Cantona lay not just in his achievement, but also the controversy. Like another famous No. 7 at Manchester United who courted headlines off the pitch as much as on it, Cantona's misdemeanours did not detract from his legacy; they cemented it. Cantona's popularity with supporters is explained very simply: he was one of them. Here was a superstar, but with the flaws of Everyman laid proudly bare for all to see.

Never were those flaws more exposed than at Selhurst Park on 25 January 1995. Cantona's acrobatic assault on Matthew Simmons provoked one of the longest bans for an on-pitch offence in the history of English football, and created a media circus the like of which the sport had never witnessed. Moreover, it threatened to force Cantona's departure from England in the same manner in which he had left France, ignominy trumping all else. Had this happened, Cantona's reputation at Old Trafford would have been very different.

Ferguson risked his own reputation over Cantona, but also acceded to him. This is captured in one memorable Steve Bruce anecdote. The squad were invited to Manchester Town Hall for a civic reception, and required to wear club suits. Cantona turned up wearing flip-flops, ripped jeans and a long, multi-coloured coat. As captain, Bruce was instructed to tell the manager that several players weren't happy with Cantona's appearance, believing it to be disrespectful.

'Fergie's on the red wine,' Bruce recalls. 'He puts down his glass, looks over at Eric. "Tell them from me, Steve," he says, "that if they can play like him next year, they can all come as fucking Joseph too."'

So when Cantona did step out of line so spectacularly in January 1995, Ferguson inevitably felt let down and wrestled with his own moral compass as well as what was best for Manchester United. In sticking by his man, Ferguson doubled down his trust in an enigma when others in his position would have taken an alternative – and easier – route. It proved to be a masterstroke.

For all the focus on Cantona during the 250 days between kung-fu kick and return to the pitch, Manchester United changed too. Ferguson started an evolution that began with a mini-revolution: senior players were sold but not replaced, while extraordinary faith was placed in a crop of prodigious young talent. During that summer, with Manchester United neither the reigning Premier League nor FA Cup champions, Ferguson would have his judgement called into question. The great manager even admitted to doubting himself. That didn't happen often.

The 'Class of 92', as they would be nicknamed in hindsight, were already on the fringes of United's first team when Cantona assaulted Simmons, but Ferguson brought them to the front and centre of his vision in the Frenchman's absence.

Cantona's role in that process has been too easily overlooked. His ban enabled him to play tutor and mentor to a wonderful generation of academy graduates. In turn it helped establish Ferguson's first dynasty as Manchester United manager.

'He changed the mentality and changed the way of everything,' Peter Schmeichel said. 'All the kids we've seen grow up with Manchester United from that period, they've really benefited from that and you could go and speak to

David Beckham, Gary Neville and Paul Scholes about him. They will always point to him, as he was the guy.'

It is wonderfully fitting that Cantona's first game back, against Liverpool at Anfield, was the first match in which all six of the 'Class of 92' appeared in a Manchester United shirt: Gary Neville, Phil Neville, Nicky Butt and Ryan Giggs as starters, David Beckham and Paul Scholes as substitutes.

This is the story of Cantona's lasting impact on Manchester United, told through the 250 days between assault and comeback. A man whose temperament was questioned when he signed ultimately failed to escape his imperfections. But rather than erode his and Ferguson's legacy, it only helped to define both.

DAY 1

*'Go on, Cantona,
have an early shower'*

At 8.57 pm, Steve Lindsell got the shot.

Lindsell had gone to Selhurst Park on a Wednesday evening to watch Manchester United try to move to the top of the Premier League and witness the third anniversary of Eric Cantona's arrival in English football through the lens of his camera. He was positioned on the touchline, primed. He would hope to sell a few choice photos – a goal celebration, frustration etched onto a contorted face, a manager thrusting his hands in pockets to protect against the cold January night – to several media outlets.

Right place, right time. Midway through the second half, Lindsell hurriedly clicked his shutter and took the photos that captured the most outrageous moment of the Premier League's first decade. The most famous footballer in the land had both feet off the ground. One was planted into the chest of a supporter. Around him, fans who had rushed to the ground after work, or paced the same walk from their homes as they had done a hundred times before, watched on. Just another home game had become a match they would never forget.

'I snapped, and snapped again,' Lindsell said. 'I thought I had a good picture but couldn't imagine the impact it would have. I went to my van outside Selhurst Park, printed the roll, which must have taken me 15 to 20 minutes, then sent the pictures. It was only the day afterwards that all hell broke loose.'

Before the 48th minute Cantona had been a passenger in an uneventful game. Palace, just outside the relegation zone on goal difference, had broken up play effectively and limited Manchester United to a series of half chances. This was largely due to the man-marking job done on Cantona by Palace central defender Richard Shaw, who had been instructed by manager Alan Smith to stay touch-tight to the Frenchman.

Smith and Shaw would later insist that the defender was merely doing his job, but Cantona spent the first half complaining about the physical treatment that referee Alan Wilkie had either failed to spot or chosen to ignore. The reality is that Shaw left his foot in on more than one occasion to both put Cantona off his game and try to rile the Frenchman. It was common practice at the time; the hallmarks of the old First Division hadn't quite been erased.

Wilkie remembers Cantona chastising him as the players left the field at half-time – 'No yellow cards!' – and the Frenchman repeating the message as the players waited in the tunnel to come back out for the second half. But, as ever, it was Ferguson's message that most stuck in Wilkie's mind. 'Why don't you do your fucking job?' was the Manchester United manager's presumably rhetorical question. This was par for Ferguson's course.

What is certainly true is that Ferguson had spoken to Cantona in the dressing room at half-time to warn him not to get involved in Shaw's games. 'Don't get involved,' he quotes himself as saying in his autobiography. 'That is exactly what he wants. Keep the ball away from him. He thinks he is having a good game if he is tackling.'

As an experienced – and very capable – central defender, seeing Cantona's frustration was only likely to make Shaw step up his strategy. You could hardly blame him. Palace could not hope to contend with United on ability.

'It was all Shawsy's fault as well,' Shaw's teammate John Salako later said with his tongue inserted in cheek. 'Richard was the best man-marker ever. He had a job to do on Eric and he did it so well Eric got so frustrated he literally booted Shawsy up the arse. Eric lost the plot.'

Three minutes into the second half, Peter Schmeichel launched a goal kick forward and Shaw and Cantona clashed again. Shaw was certainly the first to commit an offence – the linesman flagged to indicate as such – but it was Cantona's kick-out at Shaw that earned the wrath of the officials. It clearly constituted violent conduct, and Wilkie was left with no choice but to show Cantona a red card. On the touchline, Ferguson was incandescent with anger.

Later, in court, Cantona would accept Wilkie's decision to send him off but complained at his treatment by Shaw. 'In my opinion, his decision was correct,' he said in a statement read out by his barrister David Poole, 'although I had been repeatedly and painfully fouled in the course of the match.'

One of the direct results of the Cantona incident was that the rule was changed regarding post-red card events. Until the end of the 1994/95 season a player in English football would leave the field at the nearest point following their dismissal. Then followed what was a potentially long walk around the perimeter of the pitch to the tunnel, often passing large swathes of opposition supporters who had free rein to offer their own personalised farewell messages. From August 1995 onwards, players left the field in a direct line towards the tunnel. In hindsight, it is extraordinary that it was ever different.

It does not condone Cantona's subsequent actions, but the atmosphere at Selhurst Park was notoriously raucous and there is no doubt that any opposition player making the walk in front of the Main Stand would have faced many hundreds of taunts and foul-mouthed tirades.

But for Cantona, that abuse was worse than usual because of who he was, where he came from and which team he played for. Twice Cantona can be seen looking up to the stands in response to particular fans, but after a momentary pause he walks on.

'It wasn't just the tackles and shirt pulling he had to deal with that night that pushed him over the edge,' said then-teammate Gary Pallister in 2015. 'It was the culmination of a lot of abuse Eric had to put up with at every ground he went to.

'You wouldn't believe the kind of vile verbal abuse that was directed at him when we arrived at opposition grounds and got off the bus. Even when we went to the horse races, Eric couldn't escape it. I remember at one race meeting he was being spat on from a balcony in the enclosure above where we were standing. He was a target, there was no doubt about it.'

One of those supporters delighting in Cantona's ignominious and premature departure from the pitch was 20-year-old Matthew Simmons. Eye-witnesses said that Simmons had rushed down 11 rows of the Main Stand in order to get as close as possible to the Frenchman to abuse him, though Simmons would later claim that he was merely leaving his seat to visit the toilet.

The language Simmons used is also open to interpretation. Rather comically, he claimed to police in a follow-up interview that he had used the words 'Off, off, off. Go on, Cantona, have an early shower.' A slightly different account was heard in court by a witness attending the game as a neutral, and who quoted Simmons as shouting, 'You fucking cheating French cunt. Fuck off back to France, you motherfucker. French bastard. Wanker.'

It is worth noting that the court sided with the witness and that Simmons's evidence was clearly unsound, to the extent that even Cantona's prosecutor Jeffrey McCann fully agreed on that point. It later transpired that Simmons had a conviction for assault with intent to rob and was a British National Party and National Front sympathiser. There is also a theory that Simmons was not even a Crystal Palace supporter, but a Fulham fan who for some reason had chosen to attend the game. On that point, the truth will surely never be known.

Cantona had been subjected to a series of racist taunts and the strongest verbal abuse from someone intent on provoking a reaction. If Shaw was the star in Act 1 of *The Temptation of Cantona*, Simmons took over the role in Act 2.

Simmons would cause greater controversy having been found guilty of using threatening words and behaviour during the Cantona incident, earning him a £500 fine and a 12-month football banning order. When he appeared for sentencing, Simmons leapt over the bench and kicked and punched the counsel for the prosecution. It earned him a seven-day prison sentence for contempt of court. As he was led away, Simmons shouted a final parting message: 'I am innocent. I swear on the Bible. You press. You are scum.'

Whatever was said, Cantona's reaction was shocking. Pausing for a second to identify his target, the forward launched a flying kick at Simmons's chest and connected emphatically. Falling awkwardly to the floor – as is inevitable when you have propelled yourself near horizontally in such a manner – Cantona then waded in with multiple punches as Simmons fought back. Around them, Palace supporters watched on in astonishment and fear.

Cantona's teammate Paul Ince also got involved; scalded with hot tea thrown from someone in the crowd, he responded with punches of his own. It was Manchester United's kit man Norman Davies, tasked with escorting Cantona to the tunnel, who eventually dragged the Frenchman away with the help of a steward. Schmeichel raced over to try to calm Cantona down. It is interesting to see the goalkeeper pointing at the Palace support in an accusatory manner even in the midst of what had just occurred.

Back at the scene of the fight, Manchester United players gathered near the home supporters to vent their displeasure at the abuse that they believed had been responsible for sparking the furore. In front of them, a row of stewards wearing hi-vis jackets provided a human barrier between fans and players. The entire incident lasted seven seconds. Its ramifications would last for years.

'I just stood there transfixed,' Pallister told the *Manchester Evening News*. 'I was in total disbelief at what I'd seen. I just couldn't believe it. I can remember seeing Norman Davies attempting to stop Eric beating the living daylights out of the fan. Thank goodness he managed to pull him away.'

Kitman Davies deserves great credit for his pacifying role. Having eventually frogmarched – weak pun unintended – Cantona down the touchline without further incident and got him into the safety and sanctity of the away dressing room, Davies's job was not finished. He guarded the door from the inside, blocking a still irate Cantona from breaking out and continuing the altercation.

'He was furious,' Davies recalled. 'He wanted to go back out again. I locked the door and told him, "If you want to go back out on the pitch, you'll have to go over my body and break the door down."'

Having finally relented, Cantona drank a cup of tea that Davies had made for him and went for a shower. United's kitman had prevented a dire situation getting even further out of hand. He would thereafter be known as 'Vaseline' among the players, having seen Cantona slip out of his grasp to kick Simmons.

The first official reaction to the incident came from Chief Superintendent Terry Collins, who said that Cantona and Ince would be allowed to travel home but should expect to be called to police interview within the next 48 hours. 'I've never seen anything like it in my life,' Collins said. 'There could have been a riot.' On that point, it was hard to disagree.

That same evening, the Football Association issued its own statement: 'The FA are appalled by the incident that took place by the side of the pitch at Selhurst Park tonight. Such an incident brings shame on those involved as well as, more importantly, on the game itself.

'The FA is aware that the police are urgently considering what action they should take. We will as always cooperate in every way with them. And as far as the FA itself is concerned, charges of improper conduct and of bringing the game into disrepute will inevitably and swiftly follow tonight's events. It is our responsibility to ensure that actions that damage the game are punished severely. The FA will live up to that responsibility.'

Ferguson's reaction was altogether more interesting, not least because he had not seen the full extent of the incident from his vantage point and had been given mixed messages about what had taken place. A number of Manchester United players have recalled their surprise at Ferguson's composure in the dressing room after the match, barely focusing on the incident but instead castigating his defenders for allowing Gareth Southgate to score a late equaliser. That gives some credence to the theory that United's manager was not fully aware what had happened. It would have been a brave player to have spoken up to explain.

Ferguson's initial anger was at Cantona's stupidity in ignoring his half-time advice. 'Not for the first time, his explosive temperament had embarrassed him and the club and tarnished his brilliance as a footballer,' Ferguson wrote in *Managing My Life*. 'This was his fifth dismissal in United colours and, in spite of all the provocation directed at him, it was a lamentable act of folly.' That description became mistakenly attributed to the kung-fu kick at Simmons; it was actually in reference to the kick on Shaw.

Initially – and, his critics might say, typically – Ferguson blamed the referee. Alan Wilkie had also not seen the incident, although he was informed post-match of the precise details and stayed late at the ground to assist with the initial inquiries. He was met by a furious Ferguson, who told him, 'It's all your fucking fault. If you'd done your fucking job this wouldn't have happened.' It is unclear whether Ferguson was again referring to the red card or the post-sending-off events, but a police officer eventually had to force Ferguson out of Wilkie's dressing room.

Having flown back to Manchester late that night, Ferguson rejected the advice of his son Jason to watch what he described as a 'karate kick' and instead endured some broken sleep. By

4 am he had risen, and by 5 am was ready to watch the footage. 'Pretty appalling,' is the only description that Ferguson offered.

Ferguson's anger with Cantona reflected his disappointment that he had been so let down by a player in whom he had bestowed considerable faith. Manchester United had been widely derided for taking a chance on the *enfant terrible*. If Cantona's performances in his first two seasons had proved Ferguson right, here was the sting in the tail.

Manchester United's manager couldn't say that there had been no warning signs. When playing for Auxerre, Cantona punched teammate Bruno Martini after a disagreement. During a charity match in Sedan for victims of an earthquake in Armenia, he kicked the ball into the crowd, threw his shirt at the referee and stormed off the pitch. In September 1988 he called France national team coach Henri Michel 'a bag of shit' in a post-match interview and was banned from playing for the national team until after Michel's eventual sacking.

In 1991, when playing for Nîmes against St-Étienne, Cantona threw the ball at the referee and was given a four-game ban. When hauled in front of a disciplinary commission to explain himself and be told that other clubs had complained about his behaviour, Cantona approached the face of each member of the panel and called each of them an idiot in turn. The ban was promptly extended to two months.

That ban led to Cantona retiring from football at the age of 25, but he was talked round by Michel Platini, who believed that such a talent was too big a loss for the national team. It was Platini who persuaded Cantona to consider a move to England, having burned his bridges in Ligue 1.

If Ferguson's aim was to smooth the roughest edges of Cantona's ill-discipline, he barely managed it. Six months after joining United, Cantona was found guilty of misconduct and fined £1,000 after Leeds United fans accused him of spitting at them. Cantona claimed that he had spat at a wall. The disciplinary commission certainly agreed that there were mitigating circumstances, Cantona having been subjected to constant abuse from Leeds supporters.

In 1993/94, his first full season at Old Trafford, Cantona was sent off twice in the space of four days against Arsenal and Swindon. The first dismissal was for a stamp on the chest of John Moncur, the second for two yellow cards. The accusation against Ferguson's United was that they were becoming undermined by their own indiscipline. For better and worse, the players were following Cantona's lead.

Matters deteriorated even further in September 1994 in Galatasaray's Ali Sami Yen Stadium, a daunting atmosphere for any player. Cantona was again sent off, right on the full-time whistle, and was reportedly struck by a police officer's baton as he headed down the tunnel. Incensed by the assault, Cantona attempted to force his way through stewards and officials to confront the police officer, and had to be dragged to the dressing room and guarded by teammates.

'Pally [Pallister], Robbo [Bryan Robson] and Brucey [Steve Bruce] had to drag Eric in and hold him there,' Gary Neville remembers in his autobiography. 'The experienced lads were going to the shower two by two so that Eric was never left alone in the dressing room. They ended up walking him to the coach to stop him going back after the police.'

This suggests two things: that Cantona's combustibility was hardly a secret to Manchester United's coaches and players, and that his anger took a considerable time to dissipate.

The uncomfortable truth for Ferguson is that Cantona was an accident waiting to happen and that the incident at Selhurst Park – while initially shocking – was not at all surprising. Manchester United's manager backed himself to curb such 'over-enthusiasm' but was not successful, even if he rightly considered that Cantona's quality outweighed the pitfalls.

In an interview with the *Observer* in 2004, Cantona – perhaps unwittingly – alluded to the inevitability of such incidents and his own lack of control. 'If I'd met that guy on another day, things may have happened differently even if he had said the same things. Life is weird like that. You're on a tightrope every day.'

Further evidence arrives in another Cantona quote, this time on the subject of being challenged. 'I want to be like a gambler in a casino who can feel that rush of adrenaline not just when he's on a roll, but all of the time,' he said. 'He gambles because he needs that buzz, he wants to experience it every moment of his life. That's the way I want to play.'

This is the definition of playing on the edge, with every extreme element of the psyche bubbling just beneath the surface. It is a style that is rarely admitted to by sportspeople, for whom the typical strategy to achieve excellence is to rely upon an inner calm that enables composure in the crunch moments.

Cantona was a team player and very rarely selfish in possession of the ball, and yet he says that penalties – football's most individual moment – were his ultimate buzz because they offered him a few seconds during which all eyes were on him to perform. He was driven to achieve, not necessarily to help the team or for personal glory, but through an addiction to the feeling of displaying immense skill and entertaining spectators in doing so.

That might sound peculiar, but it's actually a persuasive argument. Becoming a professional footballer and maintaining your fitness and level of performance is incredibly hard. Dragging yourself through such physical and mental exhaustion for neither money nor love but to satisfy an addiction makes some sense. After all, many retired players speak of their propensity to succumb to other addictions because of their need to recreate football's adrenaline rush.

Cantona sat at the extreme end of that spectrum. Anything that stopped him playing or curtailed his enjoyment of the game became the enemy: referees with their red cards, defenders with their physical treatment, coaches with their stymied tactics, supporters with their abuse. All this explains his fury in Istanbul and south London.

Cantona's desire to 'feel that rush' blended with an anarchistic edge to his personality that lay not in a mistrust of authority per se, but a need to enjoy freedom of expression.

'Above all I need to be free,' he writes in *Cantona on Cantona*. 'I don't like to feel constrained by rules or conventions. There's a limit to how far this idea can go, and there's a fine line between freedom and chaos. But to some extent I espouse the idea of anarchy.'

Rather than rules, Cantona preferred to administer justice according to an ethical code; one that his critics might argue lacked calibration. So when Simmons screamed xenophobic abuse in his face, Cantona's temper and determination to dispense moral retribution led to a spectacular assault. The accusation from Simmons that Cantona was a 'lunatic' was spectacularly misplaced.

Amid the myriad explanations for the attack, one thing remains certain: Cantona stayed true to his principles and never regretted his actions. 'I've said before I should have kicked him harder but maybe tomorrow I'll say something else,' he said in 2017. 'I cannot regret it. It was a great feeling. I learned from it – I think he [Simmons] learned too.'

Had you spoken to Ferguson on the morning of 26 January 1995, he might have had a slightly different view. Manchester United had travelled south to Selhurst Park with the chance to go top of the Premier League. They travelled back north without a victory, with potential criminal charges hanging over two key players and with their most talented attacker once again thrust into disciplinary controversy. Lock the doors and windows and batten down the hatches at Old Trafford. A storm was brewing.

DAY 3

'Good on you Eric'

Ferguson had always been predisposed to defend Cantona, because of both his extraordinary talent and his tempestuous reputation. Manchester United's manager was aware when signing Cantona that he would require a particular strand of his man-management, but he rejected the notion that the Frenchman's disciplinary problems before arriving at Old Trafford should define how he was treated.

'He had been a bit of a wayward character at his other clubs and had gained a reputation for being unruly and difficult,' Ferguson wrote in *Leading*. 'It was almost as if he was considered some sort of demon. That made no sense to me. When you are dealing with individuals with unusual talent, it makes sense to treat them differently. I just made it a point to ignore what had happened in the past and treat Eric as a new man when he joined United.'

Ferguson makes that sound simple, but the strategy went against the grain. Ignoring Cantona's rap sheet inevitably became a defence of it. During the period immediately after Cantona moved to United, the media regularly questioned Ferguson's decision to take on a player with such an explosive personality. After finishing only four points behind champions Leeds United in 1991/92 – up from sixth the previous season – United only needed a slight improvement to win the league. The accusation was that Cantona risked rocking the boat so much that it might sink.

In 1994 Sky Sports produced a video montage of Cantona's fouls and aggression set to music. It made Ferguson furious at the alleged victimisation of his player, although the reality is that United's manager needed no excuse to rail against the conduct of journalists who he felt regularly threw rocks around a large glass house.

Ferguson did not just give Cantona a clean slate; he treated him differently to the other players in United's squad. Ferguson usually maintained an air of authority on the training ground or on matchday, but would go out of his way to talk to Cantona one-on-one every day. Recognising that the Frenchman was a sensitive personality, he would talk to him about different aspects of football relating to United and beyond in order to ensure the player's well-being.

One interesting theory – proposed by Ferguson himself – is that the Manchester United manager saw plenty of his own personality in Cantona, thus giving him added personal motivation to get the best out of him. Both had reputations for explosive anger and both saw themselves as outsiders, non-Englishmen attempting to lead an English sporting institution.

The true explanation might well have been more simple than that. Ferguson, renowned as a pragmatist, understood that having bought a unique talent and personality, there was very little to be gained in trying to mould Cantona and risk diluting him. Do that, and Manchester United might as well not have bothered at all.

If Cantona's special treatment could easily have caused resentment within United's dressing room, Ferguson's dismissal of that suggestion is gloriously pithy: 'I did things for Eric … that I did not do for them, but I don't think this was resented, because the players understood the exceptional talents had qualities they did not possess.'

Whether or not Ferguson's assessment was accurate is open to interpretation. In his autobiography, Mark Hughes writes that 'the manager had to stretch a few principles to accommodate a Frenchman who is his own man and obviously has had his problems conforming', and that while 'Ferguson didn't exactly rewrite the rulebook he treated him differently'. But the overwhelming sense is that the Manchester United players understood Ferguson's reasoning. That is a tribute to both the manager's man-management and their own maturity.

It was Ferguson's special treatment of Cantona that made him so angry about the Frenchman's actions at Selhurst Park. Having done so much to accommodate him, Ferguson expected to at least be met halfway. Cantona had made his manager look foolish, and Ferguson certainly knew that this was not an incident that could simply be brushed away through clever manipulation of the media.

Ferguson's initial reaction was that Manchester United should sack Cantona. He describes the atmosphere around the club's bigwigs as 'filled with an overriding sense of doom', but also meeting Sir Roland Smith and Maurice Watkins in the Edge hotel in Alderley Edge, Cheshire, the evening after the night before. Smith and Watkins were the chairmen of the club and plc. United's share price had dropped by over 3 per cent in 24 hours.

Smith agreed with Ferguson that Cantona should be dismissed immediately, not least because neither could envisage a situation in which it was palatable for the Frenchman to play for the club again. In *A Year in the Life*, Ferguson's diary of that season, the manager detailed his frustration at Cantona's conduct:

> I have supported Eric solidly through thick and thin, but I felt that this time the good name of Manchester United demanded strong action. The club is bigger than any individual. I related that to the board and they agreed.

Ferguson had the support of his wife Cathy, forever the manager's rock, who assisted Ferguson's decision-making far more than supporters might realise. She agreed with her husband that Cantona might have to leave or risk Ferguson being seen to prioritise on-pitch success above moral decency.

Ferguson's worries were twofold. He believed that sticking by Cantona through this incident would arm United's critics with the valid argument that a sporting institution had ceded to the temper of one majestically talented player. But he also foresaw the incident being repeated, given the media storm that had raged in the hours since the assault on Simmons.

Provocation would only get worse. This was Ferguson admitting defeat in his attempt to control Cantona.

Ferguson would later recall a phone conversation with Sir Richard Greenbury – a friend and Manchester United supporter who was the chief executive and chairman of Marks & Spencer – in which Greenbury insisted that Cantona should stay. But it was Watkins who effectively guaranteed Cantona's United future. He detailed the legal difficulties in sacking the player, and pointed out Cantona's financial and sporting assets. On these points, neither Ferguson nor Smith needed convincing.

Eventually Ferguson, Smith and Watkins decided on a disaster-recovery plan. They would suspend Cantona until the end of the season and fine him two weeks' wages, the maximum available to them. They communicated the punishment to both Cantona – who acquiesced – and Gordon Taylor, the chief executive of the Professional Footballers' Association.

By lunchtime on the following day – Friday 27 January – Watkins released a statement detailing the ban: 'In reaching this decision, which the player fully accepts, Manchester United has had regard to its responsibilities both to the club itself and the game as a whole.'

The statement left open the possibility of Cantona continuing to play reserve team football, but that was quickly rejected by Taylor. 'I don't think there's any real prospect that he'll be playing for Manchester United reserves, A team or whatever, between now and the date of his commission hearing,' the PFA chief said. The Football Association quickly applied to FIFA for the ban to apply globally, and got their wish.

The speed with which Manchester United announced Cantona's punishment was deliberately designed to curtail any further investigation by the Football Association. Having been charged by the FA and subjected to a criminal investigation, United could not hope that the storm in which Cantona had been swept up would pass quickly. But by taking him immediately out of the spotlight with his suspension, the club did at least hope to limit the damage.

Leaving open the option of training matches and reserve team football was also a calculated move. Manchester United were not surprised that the FA moved to close that loophole, indeed quite the opposite. But by making the governing body take that decision rather than them, they hoped that Cantona would focus any resentment towards the FA rather than his club.

Cantona's initial punishments did not end there. The French Football Federation stripped him of the national team captaincy and dropped him for the rest of the season. Chairman Claude Simonet had raised the possibility of Cantona losing the captaincy the day after the incident, accusing his captain of 'behaviour which is against all sporting ethics' and suggesting that 'the seriousness of the situation forces me to consider this attitude incompatible with what is expected of him'. If the norm would have been for Cantona to appear in front of a disciplinary panel to argue his case for keeping the armband, the FFF did not afford him that opportunity.

In truth, the men in suits at the FFF were only too happy to emasculate Cantona. They believed that he underperformed for his country and was guilty of an unacceptable lack of respect for authority. Although the national team could easily have stuck by Cantona for an incident that happened outside of their jurisdiction, it was never likely to be that way. Cantona handed the FFF the rope; they fashioned the loop in delight.

Far more supportive were Nike, with whom Cantona had a lucrative sponsorship deal. The sportswear giant announced as early as 27 January – 36 hours after the incident – that they would not be removing Cantona from any of their advertising campaigns.

In fact, Nike delighted in the whole affair. Cantona appeared in a television commercial in which he apologised for his actions at Selhurst Park because he had failed to score a hat-trick, while the famous '1966 was a great year for English football. Eric was born' billboard ads remained outside Old Trafford throughout the ban. There is truly no such thing as bad publicity. Cantona was just as marketable in absentia as on the pitch.

If Ferguson, Smith and Watkins felt that they had gauged the length of the ban correctly, Manchester United's players disagreed. The manager recalls that the squad, who had spent the previous day joking about Cantona doing hard labour or being sent to Alcatraz, were subdued when the severity of the punishment was laid bare. Ferguson concedes that he handled the meeting badly, but many of the senior professionals voiced their opinion that the club had overreacted to the incident and were damaging their chances of winning the title.

What becomes apparent when researching the days that followed the announcement of Cantona's suspension is just how quickly Ferguson went into firefighting mode. Having initially believed that sacking Cantona was the appropriate course of action, Ferguson subsequently agreed with Watkins's verdict and then ran with it. Despite feeling let down by his talismanic forward, Ferguson moved to defend Cantona at every opportunity. The most notorious quote was given to an assortment of journalists questioning whether Cantona should still be a United player: 'The league needs him. The club needs him. I bloody need him!'

And yet Ferguson harboured significant private doubts. 'They say time is a great healer and I hope the suspension does the trick,' he wrote in his diary of the season. 'But I've got my doubts.' This was all an act, but a necessary one. Ferguson knew that the media would seize upon any opportunity to find weakness within United, and that any extra criticism could destroy the already fragile confidence of some within the club. A United front – literally and metaphorically – was the only option.

Ferguson's firefighting made sense for Cantona's future too. Roy Keane insists that Ferguson's management in the aftermath of the Selhurst Park incident represented the apogee of his coaching career, and it is difficult to disagree. Ferguson put aside his professional concerns and personal disappointment for the greater good.

If Manchester United were going to keep Cantona and Ferguson reinstate him into the team effectively, the player had to feel the love of his colleagues and manager. As Ferguson wrote in *Leading*, 'Part of the way to extract the most out of people is to show genuine loyalty when the rest of the world is baying for blood.' Out of adversity comes opportunity.

One interesting aside to the Cantona affair was Ferguson's belief that there was a medical explanation for his outbursts. He noticed that Cantona's problems seemed to occur in the second half of matches, including red cards against Rangers, Swindon and Arsenal, and believed that might reflect a problem with low blood-sugar that could be solved by a half-time dietary supplement. It's worth pointing out for balance, however, that the Selhurst Park kick occurred only four minutes after the restart. Ferguson sent Cantona for tests to detect signs of hypoglycaemia, but the results failed to give any indication of an issue.

Cantona certainly needed the support of his manager and teammates, as the world's media exploded in response to the assault and his immediate suspension. The story led the BBC and ITN News the following day, and coverage of his ban featured extensively on both channels on the Friday. The *Sun*, that bastion of tabloid journalism moderation, allocated 12 pages to the story, while the *Mail on Sunday* sent reporters to

Marseille to poke around Cantona's childhood in search of an unlikely angle.

In defence of the country's newspapers, they can hardly be blamed for their blanket coverage. Ferguson's bitter response was to publicly wonder if there wasn't anything more important that they should be focusing on, but the truth is that the most famous – and controversial – footballer in the country had been responsible for the most astonishing attack on a supporter in the game's history. The story was – and in many ways still is – big news. Ferguson might have wished journalists to move on, but it was a forlorn hope.

What most annoyed Ferguson was the manner in which each of the bulletins and columns entered a race of hysteria, lambasting Cantona in an increasingly elaborate manner. The *News of the World*, which could usually be relied upon to find the most sensational angle, claimed that Cantona had been secretly treated for a speech defect that triggered his outbursts. If the story sounds comical now, Ferguson was not amused.

Cantona's story certainly entered mainstream culture. The *Daily Telegraph* ran a front-page story on players of their fantasy football game removing him from their teams en masse. Channel 4's *The Word* sent teenagers to sing outside Cantona's house holding flowers. Indie band Ash's first single from their début album was titled 'Kung Fu' and released in March 1995. It referenced martial artist Jackie Chan but the sleeve pictured Cantona launching himself into the crowd.

Predictably, former Manchester United players lined up to offer their disgust. Alex Stepney insisted that Cantona should never again be allowed to play for the club, while Shay Brennan remarked that the forward had betrayed Sir Matt Busby's vision of the game. Former manager Tommy Docherty believed that Cantona should have been sacked instantly, and criticised United for assisting the offender rather than focusing on the crime.

One of the most memorable quotes came from Busby Babe Bill Foulkes, who blamed Cantona's nationality for the incident. 'Eric is French – they are different to us and he reacts differently,' was his assessment. The irony of xenophobia – in very different ways – being used by Simmons and Foulkes should not be lost.

And then there was former Nottingham Forest manager Brian Clough, never short of a soundbite. 'I'd have cut his balls off,' was Clough's typically outspoken opinion. Again there was irony, as Clough had hit one of his own supporters who'd run on to the pitch to celebrate during a 5–2 home victory against Queens Park Rangers in 1989.

Much of the media coverage following the incident painted Cantona as a wild, uncontrollable beast, which was perhaps unsurprising given the nature of the assault, but it also reflected Cantona's uneasy relationship with the industry.

'Television stations, newspapers … try to manipulate public opinion,' Cantona said. 'I have been caught up in this process. The media have tried to influence people against me more often than I care to mention. When journalists attack me they show their true colours. They reveal their hand, and people are shocked. I'm a living witness to the fact that people are beginning to understand how power works.'

Cantona was being slightly melodramatic. The fevered media response to on- and off-pitch controversy in recent seasons – Luis Suárez's bite, John Terry and Wayne Bridge's non-handshake, Andy Gray and Richard Keys's sackings – indicates a tendency towards sensationalist coverage, albeit one that is reflected in the appetite of the readership. Cantona might conclude that the reaction was hysterical and hyperbolic, but it's a response that seems vaguely misplaced.

If Cantona was subject to the most blinding media spotlight, Ferguson did not altogether escape the glare. Manchester United's manager had steeled himself for criticism, having taken a chance on Cantona and been unable to control the extremes of the Frenchman's temper, but the self-congratulatory tone of newspaper columnists delighting in telling Ferguson that they had warned him what would happen was hard for United's manager to take. Having witnessed these journalists at close quarters, Ferguson believed them to be guilty of gross hypocrisy.

Yet Cantona and Ferguson only represented one side of the story, and the tabloid media was desperate to make money off the other side. Perhaps predictably, the *Sun* tempted Simmons into selling his story for a fee reported to be between £20,000 and £80,000.

Despite the police report that Simmons had suffered only minor bruising and certainly no lasting damage, the *Sun* dialled the hyperbole up to 11. 'Cantona's boot slammed into my heart,' read their front-page headline, a laughable exaggeration.

'I could see the whites of his eyes – there was total rage in them,' reads Simmons's quasi-poetic account. 'I reeled back unable to believe what was happening: I was being attacked by one of the biggest soccer stars in the world. There were nearly 20,000 people at Selhurst Park, but for those few seconds there might have only been two.' The poetry becomes slightly lost when you add that one of those two was screaming 'Fuck off back to France, you motherfucker' at the other.

Simmons's story does not end happily. He quickly regretted selling his story to the *Sun* after the backlash that followed, and his address was eventually discovered by militant Manchester United supporters. That forced Simmons to live in his mother's house, and he suffered alienation from friends and family who refused to talk to him after the incident and subsequent revelations about his character.

In 2007 Simmons was tracked down by *So Foot* journalist Marc Beaugé and interviewed. His simple assessment is tinged with tragedy: 'I was young and a bit of a cretin. But I had a really shitty time afterwards. I lost my job. Cantona played again; I was as low as I could be.'

Despite the tidal wave of media criticism, the most interesting aspect of the coverage was the swell of sympathy for Cantona that followed the initial, predictable outrage. Although all were agreed that the kung-fu kick was an unacceptable reaction and that significant punishment was merited, the case provoked questions about the treatment of celebrities.

Simmons's provocation had been so hateful, and delivered from such close quarters, that some commentators felt that the whole affair should draw a line in the sand. Sporting rivalry was something to be celebrated, certainly, but buying a match ticket did not confer a right to deliver xenophobic or personal abuse.

'When Cantona went into the crowd to sort that fella out who was giving it to him, I reckon most of the professionals were thinking, "Good on you Eric,"' wrote former Liverpool striker Robbie Fowler in his autobiography, proof that the issue could cross the battle lines of football rivalry.

Andy Townsend, then a midfielder at Aston Villa, was far more candid. 'I don't feel an ounce of pity for that bastard supporter,' he said. 'I bet his arsehole dropped on the floor when Eric came over.' The notion that celebrity status came with an acceptance of such treatment was being debunked by those within the game. Cantona was guilty only of giving in to a temptation that his peers had resisted. The line between criminal and martyr was becoming blurred.

Within the media itself, the most strident defence came from Richard Williams, writing in the *Independent*: 'You didn't have to look very long and very hard at Simmons to conclude that Eric Cantona's only mistake was to stop hitting him. The more we discovered about Mr Simmons, the more Cantona's assault looked like the instinctive expression of a flawless moral judgement.'

Williams was joined by cult broadcasters Danny Kelly and Danny Baker on *606*, BBC Radio 5's Saturday phone-in show. Kelly stated that he would give Cantona an immediate pay rise, while Baker said that the media and football authorities were way off-kilter in their outraged reaction.

Perhaps the most level-headed reaction – surprising, given his notoriously unsuccessful predictions – came from Brazilian legend Pelé, speaking in his capacity as Brazil's sports minister: 'He's a human being like everyone else. I think he's made a mistake, [but people act] like this is the worst case in the world. He has to be punished but not, as I understand a lot of newspapers say, banished from football.'

The reaction from Manchester United supporters was far more predictable. Spurred on by Ferguson's insistence that the club must support their star throughout the duration of his ban, the club's next home game (a 5–2 home victory over Wrexham in the FA Cup third round) was marked by chants in adoration of Cantona, while children had their faces painted with messages of love to the Frenchman. Outside the ground, opportunistic merchandise sellers exploited their goldmine: T-shirts, scarves and hats with Cantona-related slogans. It was as if Cantona were absent through serious illness, not penance.

One lesser-known anecdote about Cantona in the days that followed his club ban – and you can understand why Manchester United wanted to keep it quiet – concerned an incident in Guadeloupe. After travelling to Paris to film an advert, United felt it sensible for Cantona to leave the country and escape the media scrutiny. The plan could not have been less successful.

Terry Lloyd, a broadcast journalist for ITN, was sent to Guadeloupe to attempt to secure an exclusive interview with Cantona. Lloyd approached the player in the hotel complex where the player was staying with his wife and their child, but Cantona understandably refused and asked the hotel's security staff to remove Lloyd from the premises.

The following morning Lloyd followed Cantona to the beach with a film crew and started preparing to record him, shouting questions in his direction. It was a morally dubious approach, given that Cantona's wife was pregnant and that he had travelled to the other side of the world precisely to escape cameras and microphones. But Lloyd was only following his orders.

When Cantona intercepted the cameraman and again called security, a scuffle ensued. It was at this point that Cantona, according to Lloyd, launched a kick at him that was remarkably similar to the assault on Simmons. 'I'm going to kill you,' was his threat to Lloyd, according to the journalist's account.

The local police eventually confiscated the ITN tape and gave it to Cantona, but Lloyd was left with fractured ribs and cartilage damage. Even if the strategy to follow Cantona was questionable, his violent reaction was extraordinary. The Frenchman was incredibly fortunate that the incident occurred outside Britain, and that it took place in an age before smartphones. Had the story been reported in the UK media and Cantona faced further criminal proceedings, his time in English football would surely have been over.

Back in England, Manchester United had rebounded on the pitch but were struggling to manage the storm of controversy. Their title odds had dropped from 7/2 to 9/2, favourites to joint-favourites, and their share price was still falling. Common assault charges awaited Cantona upon his return, and his club were deep into firefighting mode. But things were about to get a whole lot worse.

DAY 6

*'When someone is doing
well we have to knock
them down'*

Manchester United's players and supporters were surprised at the length of ban handed down by United to Cantona, but it was a calculated move on the part of the club. The Football Association's chief executive Graham Kelly had already intimated that Cantona would be in line for a severe reprimand, but on the day after the incident he left open the idea of leaving the ball in Manchester United's court.

'I gave a clear indication at the start of the day that we expected Manchester United to come out strongly and unequivocally,' Kelly said. 'We understand that they are going to do that. We are confident that Manchester United will meet their responsibilities, not just to their own club but to the widest interests of the game.'

Ferguson, Smith and Watkins believed that by suspending Cantona from matches until the following season they could dissuade the FA from increasing the ban, and Ferguson in particular thought that the club had done enough. In *Managing My Life* he claims that phone calls between United and the FA before Cantona's disciplinary hearing substantiated this assumption. The club ban would be sufficient, and any additional ban imposed would be permitted to run concurrently with the club's punishment.

Instead, having been summoned to a hearing at Sopwell House near St Albans, Cantona was given two hours to answer a number of questions on the incident and offer an explanation for his actions. A panel of Geoffrey Thompson JP, Oldham Athletic chairman Ian Stott and chairman of the Football League Gordon McKeag heard Cantona's case, before retiring for a further few hours to decide the player's fate. Their decision was to effectively double the length of Cantona's ban and fine him a further £10,000 for bringing the game into disrepute.

The FA's statement read:

The members of the FA Commission are satisfied that the actions of Eric Cantona following his sending-off at Crystal Palace in the Manchester United match on 25th January brought the game into disrepute. Eric Cantona has therefore been in breach of FA rules.

After taking into consideration the previous misconduct of Eric Cantona, the provocation he suffered, the prompt action taken by Manchester United, Eric Cantona's expression of regret to the Commission, the apologies he conveyed to those affected and the assurances he gave to his future conduct, the members of the Commission decided that Eric Cantona should be suspended forthwith from all football activities up to and including 30th September 1995 and in addition fined £10,000.

Manchester United – and Cantona – were stunned. Ferguson felt that the club could not have left the punishment solely to the FA, for doing so would be an abdication of responsibility. But he believed that the FA had coerced the club into a severe punishment on the understanding that it would be sufficient to avoid additional penalties.

Ferguson also pointed out the hypocrisy of the ban, citing an article he had read in the *Guardian* about a non-league footballer who had jumped into the crowd and broken the jaw of a supporter. He received a two-week suspension from the FA. Cantona, Ferguson felt, was paying for his fame.

But it could have been far worse for Cantona. Kelly confirmed later that a lifetime ban had been considered, then rejected, partly on the basis of the questionable logic that a footballer has a short career span, so a life ban would be unfair.

Beyond the waffle and rhetoric of the FA's statement, there were two obvious reasons for Cantona feeling the full force of English football's governing body. The first refers back to his being stripped of the France captaincy, namely the mutual mistrust between Cantona and authority figures. Cantona barely bothered to hide his contempt for the 'suits'. His behaviour had given them the perfect opportunity to hang him out to dry.

But we must also consider where English football was in the mid-1990s. The Premier League was formed principally as a strategy from the biggest clubs to gain a greater slice of revenue, but in some ways it was also in the interest of the game to rebrand the old Division One. The 1980s represented a nadir for football in the UK: organised hooliganism was rife and English clubs had been banned from European competition for five years following the Heysel disaster in 1985. Law-abiding match-going supporters, who made up the vast majority, had been unfairly tarred with the same brush as the hooligans by both politicians and the police, creating a toxic vacuum of trust between fans and the authorities.

In these circumstances, the FA were always likely to clamp down on anything that resembled the 'bad old days' after the formation of the Premier League, their bright new dawn. This incident undoubtedly was shocking in and of itself, but position it within a climate of fear that hooliganism could easily return and the FA's reaction is less surprising. Cantona can reasonably plead that he was used as a test case and made an example of, but he should not have been surprised.

It is also worth putting Cantona's ban in the context of today's game – and there is a roughly equivalent example. In November 2017 Marseille player Patrice Evra aimed a kick at the head of one of his own supporters before a Europa League game at Vitória de Guimarães. As at Selhurst Park over 20 years earlier, the suggestion was that Evra had been subjected to xenophobic abuse. The style of the kick was even similar, albeit Evra was dragged away after a single blow.

Marseille effectively sacked Evra, although the club announced that the left-back had left by mutual consent. More interesting is that UEFA banned Evra for seven months, albeit only from European club football, given the limitations of their jurisdiction. That seven-month ban does not suggest that Cantona was too harshly treated.

Ferguson was furious and refused to attend the press conference after the FA's statement had been released, instead sending Watkins to face the press. If Watkins's own public reaction was admirably understated – 'A bit harsh' – Ferguson would finally make his feelings clear three weeks later.

'I don't think any footballer in the history of football will get the sentence he got unless they had killed Bert Millichip's dog [Millichip was then the chairman of the Football Association],' Ferguson said. 'When someone is doing well we have to knock them down.' It's fair to say that he hadn't yet calmed down.

Cantona's travails did not end at Sopwell House; he still had the small matter of a legal case to answer. On 23 March he and Ince were driven to Croydon Magistrates' Court to face common assault charges. The criminal case had become a circus of its own, requiring a police operation far beyond its merit and attracting a huge media scrum outside the court to welcome the pair upon their arrival. Gathering evidence and interviewing witnesses had taken the time of ten police officers, a nonsensical waste of resources for such a charge. As Ian Ridley states in his book *The Red and the Black*, a murder case in the same area and at the same time would probably have been allocated six officers.

Ince pleaded not guilty and was bailed (he would eventually be found not guilty), but Cantona pleaded guilty and was sentenced to 14 days in HM Prison High Down, a Category B facility in Surrey. As Ferguson was collecting a CBE from the Queen at Buckingham Palace, his star player was being handed a custodial sentence.

'You are a high-profile public figure with undoubted gifts,' said the chairperson of the bench, Mrs Jean Pearch. 'As such you are looked up to by so many young people. For this reason, the only sentence that is appropriate for this offence is two weeks' imprisonment forthwith.'

Cantona's barrister immediately lodged an appeal, while the initial request for bail was rejected. He spent the next three hours in a cell until it was agreed that he could be released on bail pending appeal, having paid a £500 guarantee.

In truth, Cantona's initial sentence was ludicrously harsh. Under 4 per cent of common assault charges end in a custodial sentence. Given that Simmons had provoked Cantona with significant verbal abuse for which he would be punished by law, and given that Simmons had only sustained minor bruising, Cantona deserved to be part of the 96 per cent.

On BBC's *Newsnight* programme, high-profile barrister Michael Mansfield stated that the punishment was grossly unfair, citing the case of three British paratroopers who had been convicted of an unprovoked attack and given only community service orders.

The football community agreed. PFA chief Taylor insisted that Cantona was being punished because of who he was rather than what he had done, and Pearch's choice of words when sentencing Cantona makes that hard to disagree with. It wasn't Cantona's fault that children looked up to him. And if his talent did indeed impose responsibilities as a role model that would cause him to suffer strict judgment in a court of law, shouldn't Cantona and other footballers be given greater protection from the abuse that had provoked the incident?

Within Manchester United gloom set in. Captain Bruce spoke of 'total devastation' and accused the legal system of making a scapegoat for football's other ills, while expressing his disbelief at the custodial sentence passed down. Lee Sharpe worried about Cantona's mental health – 'I just don't know if he can put up with any more' – while United chief executive Martin Edwards let the cat out of the bag about the club's strategy in trying to avoid further punishment from the FA.

'If we had known what the courts and FA were going to do to him, we would not have been so tough,' Edwards said. 'We took very stringent action when we banned him until the end of the season. We also imposed the maximum fine, but then the FA deemed it necessary to extend the ban. Now that is a third punishment – for one offence.'

While United – and others – had a reasonable point regarding the severity of the court's punishment, Edwards's surprise was misplaced. Having been the subject of an industry ban and legal charge, these two punishments were always going to exist separately. Expecting a court to consider the sporting suspension when handing out their sentence was misguided.

The most relevant reaction to the initial sentence came from Kathy Churchman, the supporter who had been standing closest to Simmons when he was assaulted at Selhurst Park: 'When I heard he was going to prison I just screamed out: "I can't believe it." I thought he might get a suspended sentence. He deserved to be punished, but not prison.' The closest witness to the event had proffered the most reasonable take.

Cantona's appeal was set for eight days after the initial sentencing. At his 31 March hearing, Cantona's barrister David Poole was keen to stress the importance of the guilty plea, his client's regret and also the provocation he had received. The custodial sentence had changed the mood around Cantona, raising questions of just how much abuse celebrities could reasonably endure before reacting angrily.

Poole admitted that Cantona deserved punishment and that his absence from Manchester United's team for a period of months would cause him to reflect on his actions. This absence would lead to far greater rehabilitation than any time in prison. He also dug deeply into the figures relating to custodial sentences for common assault convictions, arguing that Cantona was being treated differently because of who he was. That, Poole felt, railed against the very notion of the English justice system that guaranteed a fair and equitable trial for all.

This time, Poole's argument fell on welcoming ears. Perhaps surprised by the reaction to the initial sentence,

Judge Ian Davies returned to the chamber with a more sympathetic message than the one passed down by Pearch.

'We believe that Cantona acted in a way that was out of character,' said Davies – don't tell him about Guadeloupe. 'We believe that he would not have done so but for the provocative conduct aimed at him.' The prison sentence was quashed, replaced by a community service order of 120 hours.

As Cantona left court, with cameras clicking and journalists frantically trying to get answers to their questions, a group of Crystal Palace supporters had gathered nearby. 'French scum; fuck off back to France,' they shouted. Cantona's defence – extreme provocation – was demonstrated again even as he walked free from court.

Had Cantona's appeal not been successful and he had served prison time, it would surely have caused him to leave England. 'We are dumbfounded and absolutely shocked. I think people are trying to make Cantona disgusted with England and, obviously, I believe he is going to have to leave the country,' said his agent Jean-Jacques Amorfini in the aftermath of the initial verdict.

The English sporting media was less sure, but only because they saw no natural new home for Cantona. 'Clearly Ferguson is counting on Cantona's enthusiasm for English football surviving his run-in with English law,' wrote David Lacey in the *Guardian*. 'The truth is that there are not many other places the Frenchman can now go, since his latest fall from grace makes him even more of a risk.'

After the appeal Amorfini spoke again, this time laying blame at the feet of United: 'We are dumbfounded and absolutely shocked because Manchester United's English lawyers advised a guilty plea so English justice would show clemency.'

In fact, the only person we hadn't heard from was Cantona himself. He had chosen not to speak in any of the press conferences held by Manchester United or the FA, and only spoke through his barrister in court. All that was about to change, in such a way that it would make it more memorable than even the assault itself.

DAY 66

*'When seagulls follow
the trawler'*

Eric Cantona never offered a sombre apology for his actions at Selhurst Park. There were statements made on his behalf by Manchester United to that effect, often with the Frenchman sitting silent as the cameras flashed in his face. His barrister insisted that Cantona was remorseful in a statement read out in court, but again the words never came from Cantona's mouth. A cynic might remark that expressing regret during a trial is merely a strategy to lessen the likely sentence.

In fact, the only time Cantona even said sorry was when sending up the incident in an advert for Nike shortly before his return.

'Hello,' said Cantona, looking straight to camera with an unavoidable twinkle in his eyes at the mischief that was about to ensue. 'I want to make an apology. I have made some terrible mistakes. Last year, in a certain 5–0 victory [against Manchester City], I only score one goal. Against Newcastle I put the shot three inches wide of the post. And at Wembley I fail to complete a hat-trick. I realise this behaviour was unacceptable and I promise not to make such mistakes again. Thank you.'

Given that Cantona was still banned at the time, being so indiscreet in his lack of regret for the assault was an extraordinary risk. It could easily have been interpreted by the Football Association as Cantona sticking two fingers up in their direction. Moreover, Cantona was monetising his offence while still serving the punishment for committing it.

'We deplore violence in all sport,' said Simon Taylor, Nike's head of marketing. 'Eric knows what he did was wrong and we would not seek to condone it in any way.' But actions speak louder than words. Nike were delighted by the free publicity, spurred on by Cantona's continued popularity.

Cantona did at least offer a subsequent explanation for the incident, but only through insisting that it would not be repeated.

'There was a time when I would lose my temper regularly, when I felt I had to stand up and say something about the things that made me angry,' he said. 'I used to take a stand and rage against injustice all the time. Now I know how things will turn out and that has taken the fun out of losing my temper.'

It is interesting that Cantona framed the incident in this way. It certainly ruled out any contrition for the impact upon Simmons or any other supporters around him; quite the opposite. Cantona saw himself as a force for good in the incident, taking a stand against 'injustice'. There would be no repeat of the incident, he was suggesting, not because he had repented or necessarily been rehabilitated, but because he did not want to repeat it. And he did not want to repeat it because of the impact it had on him, not others.

The psychology is fascinating. Cantona was selling this as a matter of control and choice: I will not commit another crime because I don't want to. And if I don't want to do something, I won't do it. Losing his temper, to the point where he aimed a flying kick at a supporter, was described as 'fun'. Only the repercussions changed that.

Not everyone shares Cantona's theory of control. In his autobiography *Red*, Gary Neville likens Cantona's personality to Keane's: 'As with Keano, what you saw was what you got. They'd have been the same fiery individuals whether they were footballers or electricians. Some players, some people, are capable of counting to ten when they are wound up. Others, like Roy and Eric, are incapable of taking a deep breath. They are firebrands by nature.'

Neville is offering the opposite view to Cantona, where deliberate control is replaced by instinct. Cantona did not attack Simmons out of some desire to enact justice, but because he was incapable of avoiding becoming wound up to the point of frenzy.

Tellingly, Ferguson agreed with Neville, believing that Cantona's highest-profile losses of temper 'were not premeditated or in any way calculated but came from an instant loss of control'. On the issue of control, Cantona, his teammates and his manager were at odds.

Having remained deliberately silent for so long after the incident, the conclusion of the court case finally provided Cantona with the perfect opportunity to address the media and his public. A press conference was hastily arranged at the Croydon Park Hotel, where he had stayed the night before his appeal hearing.

Journalists attending the press conference expected a regulation, PR-manufactured statement. Cantona would express his relief at the result of the appeal, admit his culpability, and talk of moving on from this incident and focusing on his return. He would thank his legal counsel, Manchester United and the United supporters who had supported him ever since his arrival at Old Trafford. If there were to be any point of serious interest, it might lie in Cantona's comments on the abuse footballers were forced to endure from rival supporters.

It was that expectation of beige that made the reality appear so colourful and sent the English sporting media into a spin. 'When seagulls follow the trawler,' Cantona began, deliberately pausing to take a drink of water, 'it is because they think sardines will be thrown into the sea.'

As Cantona rose to his feet to leave the room, he thanked the media for their time. That last line was lost in a blur of flashing cameras and frantically asked questions that were in turn drowned out by laughter. Manchester United officials were left sitting at the table as Cantona left the room.

'It was an obscure thing to say,' said Maurice Watkins. 'He just does not want to stay here and meet you and answer questions because he has had enough. I think he has been under tremendous strain.'

Yet Watkins was acting; he knew exactly what Cantona had planned. The pair had discussed the phrasing of his short statement prior to the press conference, with Ned Kelly working with Cantona on the words even prior to that. In *The Red and the Black*, Ian Ridley even quotes the conversation

Cantona had with Watkins in which the Frenchman double-checked some English vocabulary with the United director.

'"What," he asked Watkins, "do you call in English those seabirds?" "Do you mean seagulls?" Watkins wondered. "Yes. And those boats that go fishing?" "Trawlers, perhaps," ventured Watkins. "And the fish that they use?" Watkins was trying to think of sprats but came up with sardines.'

The reaction from the UK media was one of outright hysteria. In the *Daily Telegraph* Ben Fenton wrote that 'Cantona eschewed discussion of his escape from the threat of jail yesterday in favour of a one-sided critique of commercial fishing.' The *Guardian*'s John Mullin – under the bizarre headline of 'Fish-quoter Cantona clucks the cells' – insisted that the statement 'required urgent clarification but there was none'. The *Sun* tastefully questioned Cantona's sanity under the headline 'Ooh-aah, it's mad you are'.

The most generous assessment came from Simon Midgley in the *Independent*: 'Were we the seagulls? Was he a sardine? What could he mean? As an aphorism it was worthy of Camus, nay Sartre. It was deep.'

On and on it went. The *Daily Mail* engaged a psychologist, Dr Raj Persaud, to offer his studious take. Persaud believed that Cantona was keeping the media guessing as his way of establishing that he was better than everyone else, reinforcing an air of superiority and an accordant demand to be heard.

At the risk of adding to this over-analysis, there are two schools of thought about Cantona's 'sardines' quote, and both are relatively simple. The first is that this was a very basic metaphor, in which the media are seagulls waiting for tidbits of information (sardines) from a famous person (trawler).

It's an attractive theory. Extend the metaphor further, and you might conclude that Cantona was accusing the journalists at the press conference – indeed journalists as a whole – of waiting to be fed on scraps rather than diving deeper to catch more wholesome stories. That would reflect Cantona's own mistrust of the media, particularly the paparazzi culture of celebrity tittle-tattle. In *Cantona on Cantona*, he accepted that the football media had a role to play in keeping supporters well-informed, but had let the power afforded to them get out of hand.

'I wouldn't say I was a victim of the process, but I've lived it and it's a fascinating position to be in,' Cantona wrote in that same book. 'The more media try to manipulate opinion against me, the more people like me. When journalists attack me they show their true colours.'

One journalist who accepted that explanation rather than searching for any quasi-philosophical relevance was Patrick Barclay, writing in the *Observer* to defend the press from Cantona's barb:

Cantona himself, with his fatuous remark about seagulls following trawlers, airily neglected to mention that the same species collects and disgorges accounts of his marvellous exploits with the ball, gratifying his considerable ego and helping to make him rich enough to afford the handsome clothes in which he attended the appeal court.

The second theory is that the words were not deliberately chosen to mean something – as per Cantona's discussion with Kelly and Watkins – but were intended to be entirely nonsensical.

'Hundreds of journalist were there,' said Cantona a few years ago. 'They tried to make this very serious, but I don't think football is so serious. The lawyer said to me, "They wait for you to say something." I could say "No" and go home. But these words, this line, it means nothing. After that, everybody tried to analyse the words, and I loved it. I could just have said: "The curtains are pink, but I love them!"'

It would have been amusing to watch the column inches devoted to the 'pink curtains' metaphor in an alternate reality. Was Cantona saying that there are certain things that you take an instant dislike to but ultimately learn to love because of their difference? Or was he pointing out that even something aesthetically displeasing performs an important function, like curtains blocking out light? Or were neither of these interpretations correct? Wasn't he simply making an important point about freedom of choice? Some people would hate pink curtains but others love them. There is something – and someone – for everyone.

You get the point. It did not matter what Cantona said, whether his words were intended to make a metaphorical point or were just nonsense. The point was that the Frenchman knew that whatever he said would be dissected to the point of journalistic farce. The more bizarre the soundbite, the longer the analysis would last.

It's hard to blame the media for lapping up Cantona's words; this was a symbiotic relationship. If Cantona got his kicks out of the media attention and used the post-appeal press conference as a spectacularly effective distraction tactic, he was also big business. The tabloid media in particular had good reason to hang on Cantona's every word. In a league in which footballers were becoming media-trained and so increasingly resorting to bland cliché, Cantona's utterances helped buoy up newspaper circulation.

But the lasting legacy of those 17 words was that they reinforced Cantona's mythical status. His reputation was created largely on account of his brilliance, and at least partly because of his disciplinary issues. But it was Cantona's personality that cemented it. Never before, with the possible exception of another United No. 7, George Best, had we come across a footballer who was so prepared to display his character off the pitch.

Until then in English football, the expectation was that footballers were footballers and nothing more. Anything that made them human, particularly their flaws, was kept hidden: political views, mental health issues, flamboyant fashion sense. Difference was something to be mistrusted, not cherished.

Here was a footballer whose press-conference demeanour was more noteworthy than most players' best on-pitch performances – and he knew it. 'It's funny, innit,' as the postman in Ken Loach's cult film *Looking for Eric* said. 'Sometimes we forget that you're just a man.'

DAY 109

'Only a fool would say it
didn't cost us the league'

If Cantona's absence from Manchester United's team would eventually cost them a successful 1994/95 season, the impact was not immediate. They won their next five matches in all competitions – against Wrexham, Aston Villa, Manchester City, Leeds United and Norwich City – and eight of the nine games following that Selhurst Park draw.

The high point came in the 3–0 derby victory over City at Maine Road, which briefly sent United to the top of the Premier League for the first time since November, thanks to goals from Andy Cole, Paul Ince and Andrei Kanchelskis.

'So far there is no need for a "Missing You Already" post-card to the Caribbean-lounging Eric Cantona,' an *Observer* piece read. In the *Guardian* David Lacey argued that the champions looked worthy of retaining their crown after their biggest away victory of the season so far. Ferguson agreed; he spoke of an 'outstanding performance' that sent a message to their likely title rivals.

United were hardly running away with the league when Cantona was banned. They could have overtaken Blackburn Rovers with a win at Selhurst Park, but even then Rovers would have had games in hand to retake their position. United with Cantona had lost to Leeds, Ipswich Town and

Nottingham Forest before Christmas, and dropped points against Leicester City, Southampton and Newcastle United afterwards. After the post-suspension mood of gloom, the spirit among the playing staff became one of defiance. 'We will do this for Eric,' Andy Cole said.

Nor should Cantona's ban be an acceptable reason for every other United player to escape criticism for the failure to win the title. Ferguson's team should have been good enough to cover for the Frenchman's absence. Blackburn's strike force of Alan Shearer and Chris Sutton was indeed brilliantly effective, and Shearer alone scored 17 league goals after Christmas, but they did not romp to glory. Kenny Dalglish's side dropped 23 points in their last 20 league games. That should have been sufficient for United, with their league title knowhow, to triumph.

United fell short because of too many sloppy results of their own, culminating in the 1–1 final-day draw with West Ham that sealed their fate. They lost twice on Merseyside to Everton and Liverpool, but drew games with Tottenham, Leeds and Chelsea at Old Trafford. Having beaten champions Blackburn home and away, losing the title was difficult for Ferguson to take.

United also had a replacement for Cantona in the team, if not his role within it. Cole had signed from Newcastle nine days before Cantona's assault, and had played once with Cantona in the 1–0 victory over Blackburn. Even in that first game, Cole had frustrated his striker partner with his profligacy in front of goal.

Ferguson made little secret of his initial desire to sign Nottingham Forest's Stan Collymore instead of Cole. Even after Cole had signed, Ferguson wrote in his diary that 'We'd set out to buy Collymore and got Cole,' having accused Forest and their manager Frank Clark of messing him about in negotiations.

'Andy is a totally different player to Stan,' Ferguson conceded. 'He operates within the penalty box, whereas Collymore drifts. I think that away from home Collymore's a real threat to anyone, but I think Cole is better at home against packed defences, which we are facing quite a lot now.'

Ferguson's prediction of facing packed defences proved true, but Cole's danger in such situations less so. After 0–0 draws against Tottenham, Leeds and Chelsea, during which United dominated possession and territory, United's manager moaned about the inability of his team to take their chances efficiently.

Cole was undoubtedly the guiltiest party. The striker scored 12 times between January and May, but five of those were in the 9–0 win over Ipswich and two against relegated Leicester City. Eleven of his 12 goals came against clubs who finished in the bottom seven positions that season. The opening goal against Southampton in United's last home game of the season was the exception.

It was in those tight matches and frustrating draws that Cantona was truly missed, not necessarily for his goals but his invention and creativity. One of Cantona's greatest weapons was his latent threat. Opposition managers knew that he was so supremely talented that two players would usually be tasked with stymieing him. His ability to drag defenders out of position by dropping deep or drifting wide would have created far more space for Cole in the penalty area.

With United only one point shy of Blackburn after the final day, Ferguson was certainly keen to stress that Cantona would have made the difference. 'No one's going to tell me, or even try to convince me, that he would not have made one goal or scored one goal in one of those three games,' said Ferguson, referring to the 0–0 draws against Tottenham, Leeds and Chelsea.

In his diary of the season, Ferguson blamed injuries for some of United's woes, pointing out that the team that won the FA Cup final in 1994 did not play together as a starting XI once in 1994/95. But there was one overriding factor: Eric.

'The Cantona incident was the major crisis,' he wrote. 'Only a fool would say it didn't cost us the league. I felt we were capable of winning the league anyway, but Eric would have guaranteed it. The decision by the board to suspend Eric until the end of the season was surely enough, but the FA's disciplinary committee thought otherwise. I think we can thank the press for that.'

If the league title slipped away thanks to United's profligacy in front of goal, the FA Cup soon followed suit after a dismal 1–0 defeat at Wembley during which Ferguson's side only looked likely to score after Giggs's introduction as a substitute.

Again, it was Cantona's name that was most conspicuous in match reports. David Lacey wrote that 'a couple of deft touches from the Frenchman might have made all the difference', concluding that 'his moment of ultimate daftness has cost United doubly dear'.

Meanwhile, Patrick Barclay again made reference to the profligacy that had undermined hopes of a league and cup double: 'Their array of non-participants, including Cantona and Kanchelskis, wearing red roses in the buttonholes of their smart jackets, watches a team sprinkled with youth batter away at the blue barrier after half-time yet fall just short of the quality needed.' Ferguson would agree with the sentiment.

If Cantona's absence from Ferguson's team caused the Manchester United manager considerable grief, his biggest fear was that his star player might leave the club entirely. Cantona's global ban made an instant departure illogical, but Ferguson had become increasingly worried that the media mania was adversely affecting Cantona's well-being and eroding his goodwill towards United.

Inter Milan had long been admirers of Cantona, and coincidentally had sent representatives to watch him at Selhurst Park on the evening of the Simmons incident. With contract talks between Cantona, his agent and United ongoing at that time, Inter hoped to make Cantona a lucrative offer to move to Serie A.

'The first idea I had, at the time of buying the club, was to sign Cantona and Roberto Mancini,' Inter president Massimo Moratti told *Corriere dello Sport* years later. 'Then Cantona did it, in London, with me present, with this kung-fu kick of the Crystal Palace fan.'

That's a nice line from Moratti, but probably inaccurate. In fact, Inter's president had told one of his aides, Paolo Taveggia, to make an approach to sign both Cantona and Ince, the two players most involved in the Selhurst Park trouble, as potential replacements for Dutch internationals Wim Jonk and Dennis Bergkamp, and the events of that evening did not alter that desire. Both Dutchmen would indeed leave Inter in 1995, Bergkamp for Arsenal and Jonk for PSV (although he would eventually spend two seasons at Sheffield Wednesday).

United chief executive Edwards told Taveggia that neither player was for sale, but agreed to a meeting. That meeting was arranged for 26 January, the day after the night before, and was attended by Taveggia and his colleague Gianmaria Visconti di Modrone. The offer, Edwards was told, was £10 million for Cantona and Ince.

By early April Manchester United feared that they were fighting a losing battle. Conversations with agent Jean-Jacques Bertrand revealed that Inter were prepared to offer Cantona five times his Manchester United salary to persuade him to sign. United themselves were prepared to increase Cantona's wage, but could not get close to Inter's figure.

There were also feelings among some key figures at Old Trafford that a transfer fee of £5.5 million was an offer worth considering for Cantona. The Frenchman was about to turn 29, would be banned for six weeks of the following season and therefore would possibly be unfit and prone to muscle injuries in the short term. There was also uncertainty over whether United could guarantee that the Selhurst Park affair would not be repeated. If such an incident happened again, Cantona would certainly be finished in England and his value as a saleable asset would fall considerably.

By 12 April the *Daily Mirror* had a world exclusive on the news that Cantona was leaving Manchester United. Above Harry Harris's story, the headline was adamant: 'I QUIT'.

The exclusive wasn't quite true, and ultimately proved unfounded, but it was closer to reality than Manchester United supporters might have cared to admit. 'We've always said that we want Eric to stay, but we want players who want to stay with us,' a United statement read. Those are the words of a club preparing for a star player to leave. The ball was certainly in Cantona's court.

If others around and above him were wavering, Ferguson remained adamant that Cantona should stay. That is not to say that he was ignoring the problems surrounding the forward's return to the team. It was the United manager who had been most concerned about those issues at the time of Cantona's punishment and it was his reputation that would take the biggest hit if the Frenchman repeated the offence. Ferguson worried about needing added security at away games and the scrutiny of the media before and after Cantona's return. If every element of the unpredictable forward's behaviour was going to be pulled apart, he could soon unravel.

But Ferguson was a realist, and knew that the potential cost of replacing a player of Cantona's quality would be far more than the £5.5m the club would receive for his sale. United's failure to sign high-profile foreign players to compete in the Champions League was already being cited as a factor in Cantona's potential departure.

Ferguson himself name-checked Ronaldo, Marcel Desailly, Zinedine Zidane and Gabriel Batistuta as players he wanted to sign but was told the club could not afford them. The demolition and rebuilding of Old Trafford's North Stand was only likely to make money more tight, so Ferguson insisted that the club do all they could to keep what they had.

If United took a leap of faith in telling Cantona and Bertrand what they could afford to offer the forward, hoping that the loyalty they had shown to him would be repaid, their approach was vindicated. Towards the end of April Cantona had informed his agent and United that he wished to stay at Old Trafford, and a verbal agreement was put in place that he would sign a new contract. By 27 April that contract was signed: £750,000 a year in wages and a three-year deal.

What is easily overlooked is just how close Cantona did come to agreeing a deal to leave. Alongside Harris's *Mirror* exclusive, the *Independent*'s Jim White wrote on 8 April that 'the next time Cantona plays, at the end of his record-breaking ban, all logic suggests it is likely to be in Italy'.

Even in the following January, with Cantona back and under his new contract, there was contact with Moratti. Inter had made a new approach, and Cantona later admitted that he spoke extensively with Moratti about the possibility of leaving for Italy. Ultimately, it was the support that Ferguson had considered so vital in the days following Selhurst Park that Cantona deemed so worthy of his loyalty. Even if Inter could pay him more, money alone didn't make his world go round.

The nature of Cantona's contract was unusual for such a high-profile player: an element of his salary would be dependent on the number of matches he played. The negotiation of that clause, and getting Cantona to accept it, was the work of Edwards.

'I played it canny: "Look, we've got to be protective towards the club here, because if Eric does anything crazy again we can't be paying big wages with him sitting on the touchline for eight months,"' Edwards later wrote in his autobiography. 'So the idea was for the new contract to be related to results. Eric would still get a wage, although there would be no monetary increase, but if we won the league he'd get a big bonus. And it would be the same if we won the Cup.

'Eric was training the day Jean-Jacques Bertrand and I were going through this new contract, and I could see that the agent was not entirely won over by it. After training, Eric arrived at my office and I began to explain what we had done; that if we lost the league he could end up with less, but if we won it he got more.'

Edwards had judged the situation perfectly. In that meeting Cantona insisted that United would win the next three league titles and the FA Cup three times too. He was chastised by his agent for weakening his own bargaining position, but Edwards had banked on Cantona's will to win and his unwavering confidence. Bertrand was left to respectfully disagree.

Another factor in Cantona's decision to stay was his community service, although that might sound somewhat tenuous. Ferguson had been worried that the punishment would create another circus around him, but the opposite was in fact true.

Cantona created his own coaching programme to satisfy the requirements of the order. He would hold coaching sessions for over 700 local children from local schools and teams at Manchester United's training ground. The children would be aged between 9 and 11, and Cantona would coach two groups per session on almost every weekday afternoon.

'The programme is football-related and takes into account Mr Cantona's skills, reflecting the wishes of the judge who made the Community Service Order,' said Cantona's probation officer Liz Calderbank. 'The programme will allow Eric Cantona to put something positive back into the community to the benefit of local children. It is no soft option. We have insisted that Mr Cantona devise the coaching programme himself.'

For a man who delighted in entertaining the crowds and inspiring people through his football, the project was the perfect way to at least partly replace the loss of competitive football. Rob Hughes from *The Times* met one of the children fortunate enough to experience a Cantona coaching session: 'He was terrific. He showed me that I could score. He told me to concentrate on one corner of the net, to aim for that, and now I score every time.'

These children talked of their excitement at meeting Cantona, about his advice for them, his hero status among Manchester's schoolchildren, and how meeting and being coached by him was the best day of their lives. But it doesn't take much exaggeration to describe those sessions as some of the most cherished memories of Cantona's career too. 'It wasn't a punishment, it was a gift,' he would later say. Having it emphasised just how much you mean would make anyone feel special.

But if that January evening at Selhurst Park had an unexpectedly positive result in these coaching sessions, it also had tragic consequences. A rivalry between Manchester United and Crystal Palace developed among supporters, who blamed each other's clubs for the distasteful events. This boiled over after the two clubs were drawn against each other in the FA Cup semi-final, to be played at Villa Park.

According to police reports, 35-year-old Paul Nixon was killed after rival supporters clashed outside the New Fullbrook pub in Walsall, a few miles from the Aston Villa ground. The police were called to the scene where two Palace supporters had reportedly been stabbed.

Nixon was actually crushed to death under the wheels of a coach after being hit on the back of the head during a brawl with United fans. The inquest heard that Palace and United supporters had traded insults about Cantona before the verbal arguments turned physical.

'I saw Paul Nixon staggering towards me holding his leg,' Stephen Carter told the inquest. 'Blood was coming through his hand and there was a man standing behind him holding a bar. Paul got to the door of the coach when another brick came over and hit him on the head. If he hadn't been hit by the brick I would have managed to help him get on the coach.'

Nixon died from injuries caused by the coach, but also suffered a fractured skull, a broken jaw and a stab wound to the leg. Ten men were eventually charged with offences relating to the incident, but all the cases were dropped on the grounds of insufficient evidence. Police blamed unofficial coach operators for rival fans meeting in the same place, something that was usually avoided to lessen the chance of trouble.

The match was still played that afternoon, but large swathes of Palace supporters boycotted the replay at the same ground. Only 3,500 Palace supporters attended – compared with 15,000 for the original tie – and a minute's silence was observed before kick-off. Alan Smith and Ferguson, the two managers, took the unusual step of going onto the pitch before the replayed game and appealing for calm.

As Ferguson and his superiors celebrated Cantona's new contract, the mood surrounding the club as a whole was far less positive. Not only had Manchester United been pipped to the league title and lost the FA Cup final, they had ended the season without a major trophy for the first time since 1988/89.

With question marks remaining about how Ferguson would freshen up the squad, Cantona's absence was not the only nagging issue. A summer of trouble was just around the corner, one in which United's dynastical manager would face serious questions about his own employment.

DAY 157

*'You have not let yourself
be affected by all this
bloody nonsense'*

G reat management is proved not during times of calm but of strife. For such a dynastical leader – only Auxerre's Guy Roux eclipsed his length of reign in the modern era – Ferguson regularly had his greatness questioned. Each time he proved his critics wrong.

In 1990 Mark Robins's winner against Nottingham Forest purportedly saved Ferguson's job before he had even won a trophy. The tale is slightly apocryphal – Edwards later said that he had assured Ferguson that his job would be safe whatever the result – but pressure was clearly mounting.

In 2002, three years after winning the treble with United, Ferguson was again doubted. Having finished third the previous season, United's then-lowest league position of the Premier League era, Ferguson's side won only two of their first seven league games and six of their first 14 to sit fifth.

'When the players of Manchester United look back on defeats to Bolton and Leeds, they will recognise that although you cannot win the Premiership by November, you can certainly lose it by then,' Alan Hansen wrote in the *Daily Telegraph*. 'Their manager, Sir Alex Ferguson, will recognise this difficult start to the season for what it is: the greatest challenge of his career.' United would eventually recover to win the title by five points from Arsenal.

Then, in the summer of 2006, Ferguson was suspected of tarnishing his time in charge with a series of strange decisions in the transfer market, abetted by the Glazer family's ownership. The staunchest criticism came from Rob Smyth in the *Guardian*. 'It is an increasingly inescapable conclusion that, unwittingly or otherwise, Ferguson is winding down, a prizefighter who no longer has the stomach or the wit for an admittedly enormous challenge which, once upon a time, he would have fervently inhaled,' Smyth wrote, also accusing Ferguson of 'shredding his legacy at every turn'. Over the next two seasons, Ferguson led United to two league titles and Champions League glory in 2008.

But if Ferguson was feeling strain then, nothing would compare to the summer of 1995. With all the uncertainty over Cantona's well-being and form when he eventually returned to the team in October, the majority opinion was that Ferguson should keep the core of senior players together, reinvest in the team and build a side that would wrestle the Premier League crown back from Blackburn Rovers.

Ferguson did quite the opposite. Key players were sold, precious few reinforcements were signed and Manchester United supporters believed their team to be significantly weaker at the start of 1995/96 than it had been at the end of the previous season. Ferguson effectively staked his reputation on three things: Cantona's successful comeback, a crop of highly rated academy graduates and his own strength of conviction. It would be the boldest move of his managerial career, one that would define his legacy and ensure Manchester United's continued dominance and European success.

Andrei Kanchelskis's departure didn't take place until after the start of the season, but it had been in the post for some time. United accepted bids from both Middlesbrough and Everton as early as 20 July, but called off the transfer after they discovered that Shakhtar Donetsk were demanding £1.1 million of the fee. Everton eventually referred the move to the Premier League, believing they had an agreement in place. On 25 August a deal was eventually completed. Everton contributed half of the £1.1 million fee that Shakhtar were owed, United the rest.

Kanchelskis could never have stayed at United – he had burned too many bridges. Ferguson was no stranger to a feud, but he saved some of the strongest criticism in *Managing My Life* for the Ukrainian winger. He accused Kanchelskis of metaphorically 'covering him in sewage' by attacking Ferguson in the tabloid newspapers while the club were still trying to recover from the Cantona incident, adding that he was a 'scowling, discontented young man'.

The dispute had arisen because Kanchelskis believed he was not playing regularly enough, but Ferguson argued that he had complained of an abdominal injury that neither physio nor specialist could detect. The insinuation from Ferguson was that Kanchelskis was manufacturing a reason to push for a move away from Old Trafford. After Ferguson fined Kanchelskis a week's wages for his comments to the media, a transfer request was handed in and promptly rejected.

Ferguson was furious that Kanchelskis has asked to leave in February, at a time when Manchester United needed to display unity, and he was never likely to forgive the winger. By May Kanchelskis's agent Grigory Essaoulenko told the media that his client wanted to leave due to differences with the manager; by mid-July Kanchelskis himself said that he 'couldn't see myself playing another game for United', and he failed to turn up for training in August. Ferguson would eventually discover that a clause in his contract meant that Kanchelskis earned one-third of his transfer fee.

Mark Hughes's exit from Old Trafford was less surprising, given Cole's arrival in January. The Welshman had been a tremendous servant to United over two spells, but had come close to a move to Everton before Cantona's ban and an injury to Paul Scholes.

Despite reports that Hughes had signed a new two-year contract with United – the striker even announcing as much to the media – confusion reigned as to whether that deal was ever done. Ferguson had certainly only been keen to offer him a one-year deal in light of Hughes's age, with concerns about his ability to flourish in a league that was getting quicker and more intense.

As early as December 1994 Ferguson expressed significant doubts about Hughes but also predicted a backlash should the player leave:

Mark has been at the sharp end of the game for more than a decade now and I have to be sure how long he can go on. You need a tremendous amount of energy to be able to play here all the time. The problem at this club is that they have great heroes and the supporters are reluctant to accept that their hero has died or gone away. But my job is to maintain a high level of success.

After the turn of the year, and a fortnight before Selhurst Park, Hughes and Ferguson had a frank conversation during which Ferguson told his striker that he didn't want him sitting in the stands the following season. His meaning was hardly opaque: Hughes would do well to look for a move that would pay him handsomely and provide him with regular football.

Ferguson was nevertheless torn. He would have been more than happy for Hughes to stay – albeit on a one-year contract. But he suspected that Hughes, a warrior of a striker, would struggle to play in fits and starts or as a substitute. Reserve football, League Cup football, 15 minutes on a Saturday afternoon – that wasn't Hughes.

But Ferguson was a pragmatist, and could only prioritise Manchester United: 'At the end of the day,' he said, 'we've had our money's worth out of him – and he's had his money's worth out of us. He had a great testimonial, has been paid a lot of money and is set for life. He never needs to work again. So we've not disgraced ourselves in any way.'

Hughes started 18 of United's final 19 matches of the season, but scored only eight times in the Premier League in

1994/95. When an offer from Chelsea for £1.5 million came in June, Ferguson had little hesitation in advising the club to accept. Improbably, Hughes managed seven more seasons in the top flight, but he never reached ten league goals in a season again.

The third senior player to leave, and by far the most controversial of all these transfers, was Ince. Ferguson had first been alerted to the possibility of Ince's openness to a move when a friend in the Netherlands told him that Ince's agent had been touting his client for a move to several clubs in Italy. As we've seen, Ince had already been part of a tentative double offer alongside Cantona by Inter in January.

In truth, Ferguson was looking for a reason to move Ince on, having become concerned by his attitude. He vehemently disliked Ince's demand to be known as 'the Guvnor', both on a personal level and as an affront to his own authority. He also feared that this macho persona was covering up a more insecure personality, although he initially forgave Ince for the exuberance of youth. 'This guvnor nonsense,' Ferguson acerbically wrote, 'should be left in his toy-box.'

But there were also fears that Ince's form was wavering. Ferguson worried that his midfielder was spending too much time pushing forward and not getting back into position quickly enough, to the extent that Ince was getting carried away and thinking of himself rather than the team.

Cantona's suspension had fuelled this suspicion, because Ferguson believed that the Frenchman's absence created a power vacuum that Ince rushed to fill. It was this purported power grab that persuaded Ferguson that Ince was not to be trusted. 'Success changes people,' he said in an interview with the *Observer* in August 1995. 'When Paul came to us, there was a big job ahead of us because of all sorts of problems in his background. But some people change with success. Some always want to go to Glasgow on holiday. Some want to go to France.'

Having had the seed sown by Ince's agent's apparent appetite for a move, Ferguson became convinced that it was the right idea. When Inter improved their initial offer to United of £4 million to £7 million transfer fee plus the gate receipts from two glamour friendlies – a particularly 1990s' custom – he agreed to the move.

'It will be Alex who decides whether we accept their offer,' Edwards told the media. 'He will have to consider how important he feels Ince is to the team and balance that with what he could do with the money we receive.' Privately, Ferguson's decision had already been made.

Ince, however, was hurt that United were prepared to sell him. He believed that he had merely taken on the mantle of leading the team in Cantona's absence, and that the failure to win the league title and FA Cup was not down to his own form but to the spurned chances in front of goal. Moreover, Ince believed he was worthy of an improved contract rather than simply being allowed to leave.

And yet Serie A was a good destination for the England international midfielder. If he wanted to feel important, Moratti and Inter were only too happy to oblige. Moratti had already called Ince 'the new Frank Rijkaard' and revealed plans to make him his new club captain. If Ferguson was not prepared to respect 'the Guvnor', perhaps Inter would. That sentence alone would make Manchester United's manager roll his eyes and whistle through his teeth.

United supporters threatened mutiny over the sale of Ince. Hughes's departure was more predictable, but viewed as a terrible PR move coming so soon after Ince leaving. In the *Guardian*, Ian Ross wrote that 'a team of dreams was being systematically dismantled'.

Andy Walsh, secretary of the Manchester United Independent Supporters' Association, reflected the anger of many fans:

Sadly, the supporters of Manchester United have grown accustomed to seemingly unfathomable decisions being made by the club's hierarchy. The club must now attempt to raise the morale of its players and restore the confidence of its fans by explaining precisely what is going on and why these things are happening as they are. At the moment they are asking people to pay extra cash to watch an inferior product next season.

On the issue of Ince, Walsh was no less vociferous:

Paul Ince is widely acknowledged as the best English-born midfield player in the country and yet he has been sold, seemingly against his wishes. I would like Ferguson to publicly explain the thinking behind this decision. What has shocked us about the whole affair is that no one at the club appeared to be telling the truth.

Ferguson had valid reason to sell each of Kanchelskis, Hughes and Ince, but their exits certainly left holes in Manchester United's squad. The trio had played a combined 133 matches in all competitions during the previous season, and 126 were starts – these were not fringe players. Furthermore, United had scored 110 goals in all competitions in 1994/95 and Kanchelskis, Hughes and Ince had scored 33 of them. Kanchelskis was the club's top scorer, Hughes fourth. Second was Cantona, who would be out until October and even then not certain to hit the ground running.

The obvious answer was to reinvest the proceeds from Hughes and Ince's sale in new players. Hristo Stoichkov and Matthew Le Tissier had both been mentioned as possible targets when the Hughes deal was being concluded, while there were numerous central midfielders linked with the club over the subsequent weeks.

Yet Ferguson had a different plan. He would promote from within. Between July 1994 and June 1996 Cole was the only first-team arrival at Old Trafford. During the summer of 1995, during which supporters clamoured for replacements and improvements, Ferguson did not recruit a single player. When that drought finally ended, it was to welcome York City goalkeeper Nick Culkin to Old Trafford on 25 September. Culkin cost the club £250,000. His United career was farcically brief: he replaced Raymond van der Gouw in stoppage time of a Premier League match in August 1999, the full-time whistle was blown seconds later and he never turned out for the club again.

Although Ferguson was restricted in the transfer market by Manchester United's financial constraints, Martin Edwards rejected that notion when Ince was sold. 'Any reference to the selling of players to fund redevelopment work at Old Trafford is absolute nonsense,' was his angry response to journalists' questions on the issue. But then Edwards himself immediately admitted that any incoming transfers had to be self-financed by sales. With a North Stand to build and a £5 million redevelopment of the club's training ground to build a centre of excellence in the pipeline, the manager could not be carefree with his spending.

But Ferguson didn't want to be. Even before Ince's move had been finalised, he spoke to the media and insisted that the reason Ince was available for transfer was because he had such faith in Nicky Butt, an academy graduate who had started 11 league games the previous season. 'I believe a midfield combination of Roy Keane and Nicky Butt will be as good as anything you will find in the Premiership,' was Ferguson's bold prediction. He conceded that United supporters might struggle to believe him.

That might have slightly underestimated the mutinous mood, a campaign among supporters and within the media that Ferguson candidly referred to at the start of the season as 'a bloody joke'. He named one of the chapters in his autobiography, which was released after the treble triumph, 'Public Enemy Number One'. Ferguson has never been shy to stick two fingers up at the doubters, before and after he had invariably proved them wrong.

First, Ferguson suffered a backlash from the fans. The *Manchester Evening News* ran a poll on whether or not United's manager should be sacked. Ferguson was angry at the paper for running the feature in the first place, but more discouraged that the majority of voters – 53 per cent – agreed that he should leave. The 20 per cent rise in ticket prices at Old Trafford was neither Ferguson's decision nor his fault, but he became the scapegoat for the fans' frustration. His key role in selling Hughes and Ince only pushed him closer to the centre of the spotlight's glare.

If Ferguson could put the worries of supporters to one side, he was more concerned by what he considered to be the evaporating backing of United's hierarchy. Before Ince's sale, Ferguson believed that Edwards had got cold feet, the chief executive having pointed out to the United boss that his assistant Brian Kidd was not sold on the idea. Ferguson later conceded that this lack of unanimity within the club had caused him to doubt whether he had judged Ince too harshly and been overly dogmatic on the transfer. He did not dwell on these doubts for long.

Then there was the ongoing issue of Ferguson's contract, and his belief that he was being underpaid by United. When Ferguson sat down with Watkins and Smith, director and chairman, to discuss the issue, he brought with him proof that until George Graham's departure from Arsenal he had been earning considerably more than Ferguson. Ferguson believed his success at the club merited him being the highest-paid manager in the country, and it is hard to argue that point.

The chairman had a counterpoint, asking Ferguson directly whether he believed that his powers were waning and United were slipping. What upset Ferguson most as a workaholic was Smith querying whether Ferguson believed his devotion to the club had tailed off. Ferguson conceded later that this particular line of questioning hurt him – and it was grossly unfair. The manager understandably took it as evidence that his bosses were beginning to be swayed by the vocal fan disillusionment.

For a while, Ferguson's relationship with a section of United's support soured. In *Managing My Life* he recalls a quote by his own chairman Smith about the grumbling inside Old Trafford: 'Mancunians are only happy when they are bringing people down. They enjoy that. They don't like to see people being too successful.' This must have fed in to Ferguson's bond with Cantona as an outsider in Manchester, whatever their individual and collective success.

These concerns that the fans and certain people within the club had about Ferguson provided the background for the first murmurings about his favouritism for Cantona and the grievances that this caused with United's squad. Ince certainly believed that the club had paid for Cantona's legal fees but not his, while Hughes felt that he was ignored after an injury in a way that Cantona would not have been.

Perhaps both players were right, but they had just been sold. If Hughes and Ince believed Cantona was the beneficiary of favourable treatment, Ferguson had hardly kept that a secret in any case. It was a deliberate piece of man-management to get the best out of a brilliant talent in a way that no other manager had. As so often, hindsight would show Ferguson as the victor in the argument.

Ferguson clearly believed that his position was unstable. On a lower salary than he would like but struggling to persuade the club to expedite his new deal, without the support of a large section of supporters and with a team that looked weaker than the previous season, it would have been easy for United to pull the trigger.

This, however, never really seemed a realistic possibility. The accusation that he was doing things for himself hurt Ferguson, as did the questions raised about his devotion to his job. But his character was such that denting him only made him stronger and more determined to fight. The determination to prove people wrong spurred him on almost as much as the hardwired professionalism that dictated he would do every job to the best of his ability until he had made it a success. After one triumph, you immediately started planning for the next one.

'We'll always be attacked,' Ferguson told the *Observer* on the eve of the season. 'As manager, you have to go inside yourself, be single-minded and get on with the job, and not let yourself be affected by all this bloody nonsense.'

DAY 196

*'Obviously we don't
want to lose him'*

After treating the media to arguably the most famous press conference in the history of English football, Cantona stayed deliberately quiet. He continued to train with Manchester United's first team, although most photos published by the club showed him training alone.

If the suspicion was that Cantona was sulking after his perceived victimisation by the tabloid media and English legal system, Cantona himself later confirmed as much. 'For a long time I refused to speak to the press,' he said in *Cantona on Cantona*. 'So many people had said terrible things about me, some of which I deserved. It wasn't that I didn't want to talk about the Crystal Palace incident, but people wanted me to give an account of myself.'

It was a wise move, and one that Manchester United were more than content with. Cantona was right that any statement to the media would have whipped up into a storm. Having been punished, and begun his ban and community service work, there was very little to be gained from anything other than keeping his head down and waiting for time to pass.

Cantona was also adamant that actions spoke louder than words. He could make false promises about returning stronger and with added hunger, but they would all be meaningless. Having been trusted so implicitly by Ferguson and given a new contract on a higher wage, the only way to prove these to be savvy decisions was to score goals and win trophies. Neither could be achieved before October.

Yet even without speaking or playing, Cantona still got into trouble. In late July, Ferguson told Cantona that United had arranged a series of training friendlies including matches against Oldham Athletic, Rochdale and Bury. Cantona was banned from playing in organised games, but within the context of training United believed the plan to be permissible.

The first game was against Rochdale, but the media got wind of it and widely reported that Cantona and United might well be in breach of the ban. FA spokesman Mike Parry confirmed by 30 July that the governing body would be investigating the incident and had written to United for clarification.

'The ban imposed on Eric Cantona said that he should be suspended from all football activities until the beginning of October,' said Parry. 'So we assume Manchester United have a plausible explanation. We'd just like to know what it is, to clear the matter up.'

Although Manchester United insisted that the matches were little more than a training exercise, played without officials or spectators and allowing an infinite number of roll-on, roll-off substitutions, they cancelled a second friendly against Preston North End on the day of the match.

By then, Parry had elaborated on the FA's concerns: 'We have looked at the details of the player's suspension and we concluded that any game against another club could be interpreted as being in breach of the ban.'

Eventually, the FA sheepishly retreated from their position. They released a statement that 'we are entirely satisfied with their [Manchester United's] explanation and we have conveyed that to the club.' In fact, the FA had been well within their rights to ask for answers from United. Ferguson was experienced enough to know that a game – even one without officials – played against another club could reasonably be considered to be an organised match. He and United were pushing the envelope.

That said, there was precious little to be gained by pursuing the matter. Cantona had only two months remaining on his ban. Having come under fire for the severity of their initial punishment, the FA risked further negative PR if they made an example out of Cantona once again.

But the damage had already been done. Angered by the FA's reaction, Cantona travelled to France and holed out there, communicating only through his agent, who had threatened in a statement that his client would refuse to come back to Manchester if the FA did not drop their threat of further investigation. If that statement scoped the FA's reaction, it was supplemented by a faxed transfer request to United.

'Eric was very upset at the recent inquiry by the FA concerning his involvement in the training session of 25 July,' stated Manchester United's press officer Ken Ramsden. 'He told Martin Edwards that he felt he had very little future in the English game and that his career would be best served by a move abroad.'

Cantona's outburst might seem a little petty in hindsight, but his concerns about a tarnished reputation were valid. He had already been dogged by his blotted copybook during his final years in French football and feared that the same would happen in England. With the highly lucrative offer from Inter still presumably on the table if he so wished, Cantona believed another fresh start might be the answer.

Ferguson agreed. 'Eric feels persecuted by the FA inquiry and it seems like the final straw to him,' said a despondent Ferguson to the waiting media. 'Obviously we don't want to lose him. We just have to hope that things settle down.'

Ferguson also confirmed that Cantona's transfer request had been immediately rejected, and in the same meeting sent a deliberate message of affection to his absent star. 'I don't want him to leave,' Ferguson said. 'I am determined that he will stay. I want him in my team and he knows that. I don't even want to contemplate a situation where he says he is going.' If the language within that message belongs in a teenage love letter, it was chosen meticulously.

In fact, it took a great deal more from Ferguson to save the day, spurred on by his wife Cathy, who persuaded him to travel to Paris when he was starting to be concerned that the situation was a lost cause. Thus began the farcical saga of Ferguson in France, tracking down Cantona.

Ferguson flew into Charles de Gaulle Airport and dodged the gaggle of journalists waiting for him at arrivals. He jumped into a taxi and was taken to the Hotel George V in the city centre, where he would stay. In his room, Ferguson received a call from Jean-Jacques Amorfini, Cantona's lawyer and vice-chairman of the French PFA. He told Ferguson that a porter would collect him from his room at 7.30 pm and bring him to Amorfini. If this already has the feel of a low-budget, arthouse spy film, Ferguson's description of the porter telling him to 'Follow, Monsieur Ferguson' completes the image.

When Ferguson finally met Amorfini, having been led through the hotel's myriad corridors, the lawyer was sitting astride a Harley-Davidson motorbike and had a spare crash helmet for Ferguson to wear. The United manager clambered onto the bike behind Amorfini and then rode through the side streets of Paris to a small restaurant with a closed sign attached to the door.

Deep within the almost silent restaurant, Cantona and his agent were waiting to greet Ferguson, who soon launched on a charm offensive that lasted several hours and would revitalise Manchester United's short-term prospects and help to define both individuals' legacies.

Ferguson had formulated his plan of attack on the plane from Heathrow. He stressed to Cantona that the FA's investigation – which had by now been dropped – was not an attack on the individual but on Manchester United's decision to organise the friendlies without the prior say-so of the governing body. Moreover, he would be permitted to play in a number of other matches before his return. He told Cantona how Watkins, the club's lawyer, had fought vehemently on Cantona's behalf over the issue.

More importantly, public opinion had shifted in England since news of the investigation had filtered through. Supporters – and not just of Manchester United – believed that having almost completed his ban and served his community service by helping hundreds of children in the local area, Cantona had demonstrated his love for the game and proved his power as an inspiration for young fans.

Finally, Ferguson told Cantona just how important he believed he would be to United upon his return. Having sold three senior players and replaced none of them, Ferguson had a vision of a new Manchester United. Young players would be given ample opportunities in the first team, and Cantona would be their role model. His professionalism, work rate and on-pitch brilliance would ensure as much.

There is no doubt that Ferguson, who had been persuaded to pursue Cantona by his wife Cathy, laid it on thick in Paris – this was a charm offensive. But he said nothing that was not true, and it worked. Cantona was impressed that Ferguson had flown to Paris just to see him, and felt vindicated in signing his new contract.

The next day, United briefed to the media that Cantona would be returning to Manchester and would recommence training. By August, Ferguson confirmed the news. 'His future is secure with us,' Ferguson said. 'I haven't had much sleep, but I'm happy the job has now been done.' Half a city rejoiced; so too did Manchester United's manager.

Whether or not Cantona was ever likely to follow through with his request to leave is open to debate. The *Guardian*'s Richard Williams certainly predicted the turn of events that followed. On the day that Ferguson travelled to Paris, Williams wrote that 'Alarm notwithstanding, it will be a real surprise if, when the season opens in two weekends' time, he [Cantona] is not still pursuing his ethereal dreams in the colours of Manchester United.'

Williams's view, backed up by simple logic, is that Cantona's transfer request was a cry for help. Having been unable to play and thus with his creativity stymied, Cantona was always likely to become frustrated by life away from the pitch. The FA's threat therefore caused a reaction not dissimilar in nature to the one at Selhurst Park, albeit using a fax machine rather than football boot to vent his building anger.

There is also a reasonable assumption that Serie A might not have been the perfect environment for Cantona – and that Cantona knew it. Inter coach Ottavio Bianchi would surely not have managed Cantona so delicately and deliberately as Ferguson, and Bianchi was sacked before the end of September in any case. Cantona would have received no less physical treatment from Serie A defenders than he did in the Premier League, and his fluid style worked perfectly against rigid English defences.

No, Cantona only wanted to be loved and embraced, made to feel special by his manager. Ferguson, the closest

Cantona came to a father figure in the game, understood that desire. Expressive shows of loyalty were the route to Cantona's heart. If venturing through a Paris evening on the back of a motorbike to a deserted restaurant was as good as a diamond ring and a dozen roses, then so be it.

Anything other than reconciliation would have been a disaster for Ferguson. Having prioritised Cantona's happiness and resolved to build a team with the Frenchman as its leading man, Cantona's departure would have left United's pre-season plans in tatters only a fortnight before the new season began.

It would also have seriously called into question Ferguson's decision to both refuse to replace Hughes and Kanchelskis and to rely so fervently on Cantona's capricious personality. It is no surprise that Ferguson made such a forthright assessment in his autobiography: 'Those hours spent in Eric's company in that largely deserted restaurant added up to one of the more worthwhile acts I have performed in this stupid job of mine.'

DAY 207

*'You can't win anything
with kids'*

It was one of the youngest teams that Manchester United had ever selected for a league game. Of the starters at Villa Park on the opening day of the 1995/96 Premier League season, four – Paul Scholes, Gary Neville, Phil Neville and Nicky Butt – were aged 20 or under. Another two in the same age bracket – David Beckham and John O'Kane – were substitutes, and Beckham came on at half-time. United were comprehensively outplayed by Aston Villa, beaten 3–1 by a team that had survived relegation by a single place the previous season.

If the game became infamous in glorious hindsight, it was Alan Hansen, speaking on the BBC's flagship football programme *Match of the Day*, who gained most notoriety. With presenter Des Lynam labelling United as 'scarcely recognisable from the team we've known over the last couple of seasons', he turned to Hansen to ask just what was going on. The great Scottish defender, tanned and dressed in a light suit and tie, had his answer ready straight away:

I think they've got problems. I wouldn't say they've got major problems. Obviously three players have departed. The trick is always buy when you're strong, so he [Ferguson] needs to buy players. You can't win anything with kids. You look at that line-up that Manchester United had today, and Aston Villa at quarter past two when they got the team sheet it's just going to give them a lift and it'll happen every time he plays the kids. He's got to buy players, as simple as that.

Hansen's comment has gone down in folklore as one of the most memorable quotes of the Premier League era, maybe even more famous than Cantona's 'Seagulls follow the trawler'. A book detailing the history of the Premier League through quotes has the quote as its title, while there is another published book with the same name. (Slightly bizarrely, there is also a book by writer Jim White entitled 'You'll win nothing with kids'. The misquote was presumably not deliberate.)

In terms of spectacularly bad predictions, only Michael Fish's 1987 insistence that talk of a hurricane was nonsense hours before the Great Storm killed 22 people and blew down 15 million trees in the Home Counties can outdo Hansen's for its lasting cultural resonance.

Perhaps Hansen was being a little spiky because he was a Liverpool legend who reportedly enjoyed a frosty relationship with Ferguson, although Hansen later completely dismissed that idea. He failed to learn his lesson, however; his article on Manchester United's strife in the *Daily Telegraph* in 2002 provoked the 'my greatest challenge was knocking Liverpool off their fucking perch' response from a clearly angered Ferguson.

But Hansen is mocked far too strongly for his 'kids' assessment. If hindsight does indeed make his prediction look foolish, which of us hasn't anticipated something that never happened? Football's inherent attraction lies in its unpredictability, even to those who can claim to have been schooled in the game. It is a mystifying, magnificent sport. Every time you think you can foresee the future, football makes you look foolish.

Manchester United were at a point of crisis at the time. That month was the only occasion on which Manchester United had not appeared in the Charity Shield between 1993 and 2002. Incredibly, it was only the second time since December 1992 that Manchester United had conceded three goals in a league fixture (the other being a 3–3 draw at Anfield in January 1994).

Ferguson himself had privately conceded that he worried that his job was in some jeopardy, failing to feel the warmth of support from either supporters or the club's hierarchy. Had you interviewed a selection of travelling fans outside Villa Park after the final whistle, they would surely have sung from a similar hymn sheet to Hansen. Supporters were concerned about rising ticket prices, but more angry that three key players had been sold with no replacements in the pipeline. Their club, these fans felt, was playing them for fools.

If Hansen did go a little too far, he was not alone. Martin Thorpe, a *Guardian* writer, reflected the mood in print from the ground, describing a team that had been 'overrun, out-thought and even outclassed'.

'Perhaps after the nightmares of Cantona and Kanchelskis, defeat at Villa Park struggles to register on Ferguson's internal scale of shock,' he wrote. 'But as an exercise in proving his point, Saturday could hardly have been worse for the United manager. Forget the loss of Ince, Kanchelskis and Hughes, he told the fans, have faith in the youngsters. Well, here was the first result of his theory: 3–1 to Aston Villa and 1–0 to the critics who warned him he had got it wrong.'

Hansen was unconvinced about Manchester United's chances of winning the league title, and his insistence that Ferguson would have to spend was proven wrong. But United's team against Villa was missing Ryan Giggs, Steve Bruce and Andy Cole, as he acknowledged. Those three would all start 30 or more of United's 38 league games.

Meanwhile, O'Kane would never play another league game for United, Scholes started only 16 league games in 1995/96 and Phil Neville only 21. So in some respects Hansen was right. Ferguson could not simply pick all of his academy crop and expect to win the league.

'That line pretty much made me, simply because I got it so dramatically wrong,' Hansen said in 2012. 'But despite being so dramatically wrong, if United hadn't won the double that year, you could still say that line now. I could have said it ten years later and it would be relevant because it is a fact, but what happened with United was a one-off. I just said it at the wrong time.'

Hansen's self-defence is valid. Never since 1995/96 has there been a team containing such widespread inexperience that has achieved so much so quickly, and there might never be one again. With transfer budgets continuously increasing and patience in managers – particularly at elite clubs – decreasing, it is easier and safer to buy ready-made replacements than promote from within. Young players make mistakes, and mistakes costs jobs.

But Hansen's – and others' – great mistake was in overlooking just how special that crop of Manchester United academy players was. The full Class of 92 (Giggs, Butt, Scholes, Neville G, Neville P, Beckham) that stayed at Manchester United long after winning the FA Youth Cup in 1992 to claim the treble in 1998/99, would eventually win 54 career league titles and amass 432 senior international caps between them.

Ferguson knew that he had a supremely talented age group passed on from his youth coach Eric Harrison. They had won the FA Youth Cup for the first time in 28 years, but even before the two-legged final Ferguson had been making plans to promote several of the side to become first-team regulars in 1995/96. After he watched the same group lose to Leeds United in the 1993 FA Youth Cup final, narrowly failing to defend their crown, Ferguson exclaimed: 'I've never seen their like before.'

'We don't like to go overboard about youngsters, but this lot are very exciting,' Ferguson said. 'With their ability and desire to play they should go far. Winning the FA Youth Cup can be significant. When Manchester United last won it in 1964, it triggered the best period in the club's post-Munich history.'

In those few words, Ferguson's vision is laid bare. His decision not to reinvest in his squad in the summer of 1995 was based on three distinct factors: a tightening of budgets at Old Trafford, an annoyance at the behaviour of Kanchelskis and Ince, two previous marquee signings, and the belief that his fledglings could not just thrive in the first team but provide the backbone for a new era of dominance. If Hansen's prediction was spectacularly wrong, Ferguson's was proven sensationally right.

Ferguson had already created a legacy with consecutive league titles, but he believed that this group of young players, if given the perfect conditions for their nurturing and development, could be the next Busby Babes. The tragedy of Munich would never – should never – be forgotten. But the perfect tribute to that fallen team was to recreate its majesty: local lads, a group of mates, a sensational football team.

Even if this new group of young players was outrageously talented, talent only means so much. In Ferguson, the fledglings had a manager who would drive them on to success by any means necessary. But they also needed a mentor in the playing squad, someone who they could look up to on a number of levels but who would delight in helping them fulfil their potential. Perhaps even a player who might be training every day but who was denied the buzz of competitive football – and so in need of a project. Enter Eric.

Cantona's immense natural talent made him the perfect idol for Manchester United's young players. There is an anecdote about his first day at Manchester United training, when plenty of the club's senior players were a little circumspect about his signing. As the squad, including some youth players, was standing around, Cantona kicked a ball against a wall, controlled it as it returned to him and then proceeded to juggle the ball in a way that left those around him astonished.

It was noted at the time that Scholes and Beckham were part of that throng. How could you fail to be inspired to become so good? There comes a point when talent becomes infectious. 'The things he tries, the others try,' said Ferguson. 'It's the way the team are playing now that's got middle-aged fans jumping about like two-year-olds.'

Ferguson also used Cantona's talent as a motivational tool for his academy crop. During an away victory at Southampton in 1993, Ferguson watched Cantona play a wonderful pass through to a teammate. Turning around to Giggs, who had just been substituted, Ferguson said sharply: 'When you reach that level of accuracy, you can call yourself a player. You're watching a master at work.'

Yet it is difficult to inspire on natural talent alone. The very definition of the phrase indicates that it is innate within you, and therefore cannot fully be passed on. You can appreciate transcendent players but can never hope to copy them. Training with Cantona would obviously improve young players' technique, but none of the Class of 92 possessed his skill. They became famous as much for their dedication to maximising their natural talent as for the talent itself.

So if Cantona's skill made him an idol of Manchester United's young players, his dedication made him a role model. 'Your colleagues are doing their best to improve themselves; it's up to you to never let them down. That's respect,' Cantona wrote in *Cantona on Cantona*. 'In preparation and on the pitch, we give our all. After the match, there will be plenty of time to relax. Before the match, your whole life revolves around ensuring the sweetest and most glorious victory.' That quote could have been printed out by Ferguson and pasted on the walls of The Cliff training ground for generations of players to follow.

Before he had even played his first match for United, Cantona's professionalism was impressing Ferguson. At the end of a morning training session, Cantona asked his manager for the loan of two players for an hour. He would delay his lunch. Ferguson agreed, and watched on as Cantona practised extra dribbling and shooting. Other senior players heard about what was going on and went outside to watch with their manager.

The message was clear. Natural skill was not something merely to be relied upon, but should be cherished and honed. That Cantona's extra session caused such surprise among his peers speaks volumes about the nature of training even within the best clubs in the land. Sessions could be enjoyable, but they were there to be endured.

'Eric is the type who doesn't say anything in training,' Ferguson wrote in *A Year in the Life*. 'He just practises and practises. He is the perfect pro. He is the first on the training field and virtually the last off it.'

Ferguson also recalled how over time the other players

would also ask for extra training sessions, starting with the youngsters but soon the entire squad, bar those like Bruce who had to manage the decline that comes with age. 'On Fridays I have to ask them to come in off the pitch,' Ferguson said. You can detect the beaming pride in those words. Management is far easier when those below you are motivating themselves.

Later in 1994/95, Ferguson went further still in praise of his French forward: 'He's the best-prepared footballer I've ever had. He's first at the training ground, he does his warm-up and then he does our warm-up. He trains brilliantly. He's a model pro, an absolute dream of a footballer.'

That attitude resonated with United's younger players. Here was a supreme talent who understood the necessity of constant hard work. Long training sessions weren't just how you improved as a player, but how you ensured that your peak could be extended. Amid the lingering drinking culture that still existed within Manchester United – and most other clubs too – in the early 1990s, Cantona offered an opposing philosophy. Football was great fun, but fun requires serious preparation.

Gary Neville remembers Cantona as a perfectionist in training. He credited the Frenchman for helping him to look better than he was, but also recalls how a mistake in a warm-up match – an unsuccessful tackle or a misplaced pass – would earn you a stare that would persuade you to work doubly hard to ensure the error was not repeated. Cantona was driving the youngsters on.

Cantona's professionalism went far beyond training drills, however. Arsène Wenger is rightly credited with transforming Arsenal through his belief in improving nutrition, diet and conditioning, but four years before Wenger was appointed Cantona was doing the same at Manchester United. He didn't eat red meat more than once a week, believing that over-consumption led to the body producing toxins that would impair physical performance. This is a move Lionel Messi made midway through his career, taking his game to even more transcendent levels.

Cantona would eat pasta once a day, and avoid fast-burning sugars that provide a glucose rush but not sustained, slow-release energy. He stressed to his teammates the importance of drinking lots of fluids and getting as much sleep as possible – he slept for at least ten hours per night. They should go out and enjoy themselves – rewards are a psychological trick to sustain motivation – but tone down their alcohol consumption.

If that all now sounds entirely logical for elite sportspeople, it was not always the case. Ferguson had already made moves to rid Old Trafford of the First Division drinking culture that had somehow still staggered into the Premier League era, but having such an influential player singing from the same hymn sheet as him made Ferguson's task considerably easier.

For a player who seemed to perform on pure instinct, Cantona was very tactically astute. In December 1994, after United had beaten Galatasaray 4–0, Ferguson came back to the dressing room to witness Cantona talking Gary Neville and Beckham through passages of play on a tactics board. In his book *Leading*, Ferguson actually credits Cantona for coming up with the tactical plan to beat Liverpool in the FA Cup final in 1996. He suggested that Keane drop much deeper than usual to try to suffocate the service to Steve McManaman. Ferguson says he had not considered that option, and that Cantona's plan was crucial to his team's victory.

Finally, Cantona's mentorship was largely about his presence. He possessed a confidence that bordered on invincibility, which cannot fail to be inspiring. It is no coincidence that this was precisely the same aura that Manchester United projected as a club during the most successful years under Ferguson after Cantona had left.

The club had other leaders for these fledglings to follow. Bryan Robson did not leave until 1994, Steve Bruce was the captain, Peter Schmeichel a warrior and Roy Keane replaced Paul Ince as the heartbeat of the central midfield. But none combined skill, swagger and sacrifice to his art like Cantona.

As Schmeichel would write in his own autobiography, 'It is my contention that Eric Cantona's importance for Manchester United must not only be measured by his efforts on the field, but just as much by the inspiration and experimental initiative.' Ferguson agreed: 'We had some tremendous young players just emerging, and Eric came at the right time for them. He brought the sense of big-time thinking, the vision and the imagination and general play.'

Cantona jumped at the chance to be a mentor and tutor for the academy graduates. Cast your mind back to his reaction to the community service, when he delighted in coaching 700 local children. This was his chance to be a role model for a different group of young people, but ones with whom he could work every day. It gave him great joy not only to witness his positive impact upon the Class of 92, but that those same players then became mentors for the next generation of young players, both at Mancheester United and at international level.

'When I see them, these boys of Manchester,' he said of that group, 'when they touch me, when they speak to me in hushed voices, I want them to go away happy and convinced that they have met a player who is more like them than they know.' The same words could be used apropos his coaching sessions for children during the summer of 1995.

It was also Cantona's chance to pay Manchester United back for their support and loyalty, and in particular Ferguson. Without competitive football to sate him, this coaching of United's young elite was a pet project in which he could make a lasting difference and leave an indelible mark on the club that always felt most like home.

The anecdotes of Cantona's influence upon their early careers from each member of the Class of 92 are far too numerous to list, but each one gives a different insight into Cantona's micro-management of their game and personalities.

David Beckham flourished when given compliments. He would stay behind long after training with Cantona to practise his free-kicks and long passing. The proudest moment for Beckham when he scored from the halfway line against Wimbledon on the opening day of the 1996/97 season was Cantona telling him that it was the best goal he had witnessed live.

For Gary Neville, meanwhile, one of the driving forces behind his early career was proving to Cantona that he belonged. When you got something wrong, Cantona didn't belittle you but inspired you to be better. 'We were desperate to impress him,' wrote Neville in his autobiography, but he would also say that Cantona was the player he would go to for advice. For all the considerable aura that encircled Cantona, he was always approachable. That is rare.

'He had a massive influence on my career as a young player coming into the team,' says Giggs, another flair player and so someone whom Ferguson wished to live under Cantona's wing. 'We struck up a good relationship and he ruled Old Trafford for five years.

'He was an unbelievable talent to play with and watch in games and training. Eric Cantona brought an extra dimension. Plenty of things he tried didn't come off, but you remember the ones that did – the flicks, the outrageous lobs. He made things look easy that weren't easy at all. Before him, we struggled to score as a team, but as soon as he arrived the goals flowed.'

For Scholes, Cantona was a tactical tutor. Scholes was an incredibly versatile player who began as a forward and eventually became an incredibly effective attacking midfielder. In his pomp, he would drop deep to pick up possession, link midfield and the striker brilliantly and find space where none should exist. He had the courage to demand the ball in tight spots, and also had a tendency to fly into tackles when frustrated by losing possession. One guess where he might have learned all of this.

Cantona did not just teach these players in training, he looked out for them as an older brother might, teaching them the ways of the world on a quasi-philosophical level. At the time, the squad had a tradition of pooling all the media appearance fees for the FA Cup final, and each player was given the chance to either take their share or leave it in the pot and be part of a draw to win the entire sum.

Most of the young players, including Gary Neville and Beckham, took their share; this was a handy bonus for those on low salaries. But Scholes and Butt left their share in. Cantona won the draw and with it the prize of £7,500. That was the equivalent of two months' wages for Scholes and Butt. Cantona gave each of them £3,750, 'because they showed balls'.

It is a happy coincidence that Cantona's first game back, against Liverpool, was the first game in which all six of the Class of 92 played for Manchester United's first team. His integral role in the development of that extraordinary generation has been slightly overlooked, has faded over time. One man who does not underestimate Cantona's importance is Ferguson.

'It is such a tonic for a youngster to feel that he has a mentor whom he can trust and who has his interests at heart,' he wrote in *Leading*. 'There is more of a natural bond between players than there is between coaching staff and players. There is a lot to be said for either picking, or being lucky enough to land, the right mentor. The best ones can change your life.'

But if Cantona helped to shape the careers of some of the Premier League's most successful players, it was a long term project and some – including Hansen – felt Manchester United were in desperate need of a quick fix.

United did respond to their opening-day defeat to Aston Villa. They recovered from a Bruce own goal to beat West Ham 2–1 in their first home league game of the season, killed off Wimbledon after half time in a 3–1 victory, held on with ten men against Blackburn after Roy Keane's sending-off and beat Everton 3–2 despite twice conceding equalisers. By the time Bolton had been brushed aside 3–0, United were second in the league and the division's joint-top scorers.

But even then, the accusation was that paper was being smoothed handily over cracks. Andy Cole had scored just once in the opening six league fixtures, but worse news was to come in the cup competitions. If a shambolic 3–0 home defeat to third-tier York City could be partly explained by Ferguson picking a weakened team, that starting XI contained

Giggs, Phil Neville and Beckham alongside Lee Sharpe, Gary Pallister, Denis Irwin and Paul Parker.

In the final game before Cantona's ban ended, United were knocked out of the UEFA Cup at the first hurdle by Russian side Rotor Volgograd, who would finish 31 points from the top of the Russian Top League in 1995. That night, even a Peter Schmeichel goal could not save them, the team departing the competition on the away-goals rule.

'Manchester United clung, just, to their unbeaten home record in Europe last night but still plummeted out of the UEFA Cup in the first round,' wrote Guy Hodgson in the *Independent*. 'It is a result that even Eric Cantona's return on Sunday will not obliterate.' In the *Guardian*, Cynthia Bateman was equally cutting: 'United looked like a team who had never played together.'

In fact, Cantona's return did help Ferguson's cause. As the days were counted down to the Liverpool game and the media re-entered frenzy mode, a blanket was placed over Manchester United's bad-news stories. What was the point in making more sweeping conclusions about the health of Manchester United when their talisman was about to return?

Everyone was waiting for Eric. An entire country anticipated the return of the King.

DAY 250

*'A Mancunian version
of Bastille Day'*

It might never have been Liverpool. When the fixtures for the 1995/96 Premier League season were released on 21 June, Cantona's first game back was scheduled to be a local derby against Manchester City on 14 October, United's first scheduled game of the month.

The home game against Liverpool was slated to take place on 30 September, the final day of Cantona's ban. But by then Sky Sports had the power to move matches for live television coverage, and there was little doubt which match they would choose. By shifting the match to the Sunday and thus taking it into October, Sky made sure that Cantona would be available.

It was never Ferguson's assumption that Cantona would start matches as soon as he was available. After Cantona's ban had been extended, Ferguson conceded that Manchester United supporters would most probably not see the forward regularly until November, because it would take him at least a month to be fully match-fit.

But after European and League Cup exits, and with a point to prove even to his own supporters and superiors, it quickly became clear that Cantona would return on an ASAP basis. Any doubts about his match fitness were eclipsed by the positive impact his return would have on those around him. Cantona's extraordinary dedication to training would clearly erase some of the likely rustiness after eight months out.

Cantona would also not have dealt well with being edged back into the team gently. It was little secret within Old Trafford that, although he had enjoyed mentoring the club's young players and had trained as if he were preparing for competitive matches, his long absence from United's team was gnawing away at him. Had Ferguson told him to stay on the bench against Liverpool, perhaps giving him 15 minutes at the end, it would only have meant further mounting frustration.

'The week before the game I spoke with him on the phone,' his agent Jean-Jacques Bertrand would later say. 'We spoke about different things, but never about the match on Sunday. It was not necessary. He wanted to play, because that is his life. The game, the field, the fans, to compete. That is what he wants.'

Had Ferguson chosen any fixture for Cantona's return, it would surely not have been a game against United's fiercest rivals. Southampton or Bolton at home, perhaps, or an away trip to Sheffield Wednesday. But Liverpool was different. A match that needed little extra to spark a flash of ill-discipline was to be the testing ground for Cantona's newfound serenity.

If Ferguson had publicly offered a staunch defence of Cantona's character and assured anyone who would listen that there would be no repeat of Selhurst Park, he still harboured private reservations. Even at Old Trafford, with away supporters absent due to the continuing building works to revamp the stadium, the atmosphere would be febrile. And what about Stamford Bridge, Anfield and Maine Road?

Ferguson was interviewed in the build-up to the match, and began by reiterating how impressed he had been with Cantona's attitude in training. Then came a very telling pause as the cameras clicked incessantly, Ferguson looking up as if choosing his words carefully. 'And, obviously … I don't think … I think there will be times where he loses his temper in a game. Plenty of players do that. But he also knows that he has got to show maturity and responsibility. I'm certain I've done the right thing in giving it a go.' There was a sense that Ferguson was re-convincing himself in real time.

In his previous appearance against Liverpool in September 1994, Cantona had been booked for a rash tackle from behind on Neil Ruddock that many believed could have earned him worse punishment, although referee Kelvin Morton had missed some rough treatment by Ruddock, including an elbow on Cantona. As David Lacey wrote in the *Guardian*, 'it was the elbow from Ruddock which lit Cantona's short fuse'.

'It'll be ten times worse than before,' said George Best, who knew a thing or two about coping with the pressure of being Manchester United's No. 7 under the blinding glare of the spotlight. 'He'll have to show to everyone, and especially himself, that he is able to face it, that he has grown up and has become a man.'

Were any other incident to occur, Ferguson knew that he, Cantona and Manchester United would be swamped by a tidal wave of hyperbolic criticism. It would not even need to be a moment of extreme violence. Commit a bad tackle, lash out at an opponent or hurl a volley of dissent in the direction of the officials, and Cantona's inevitable back-page presence on Monday morning would be given a negative, exaggerated spin. It goes without saying that Liverpool as opponents made all three more likely.

But Ferguson's main concern was the unprecedented media circus that was enveloping Manchester United. Every training session has been filmed during the build-up, and every question Ferguson fielded at his pre-match press conference concerned Cantona's return. Manchester United had even rejected a request from Sky Sports to film in the home dressing room before the match. It is left to our imaginations to wonder what Ferguson's reaction to that request might have been, but we can safely assume that he was not keen on the idea.

Cantona's sponsors were doing their bit to add fuel to the fire. 'He's been punished for his mistakes,' the message on a Nike billboard near Old Trafford read. 'Now it's someone else's turn.' The television advert in which Cantona thrust tongue into cheek to apologise for his actions in missing chances and only scoring one goal was released. It's hard to imagine that Ferguson was impressed.

The back-page headlines had become front-page splashes. Cantona's return was not just a sporting story but a matter of national interest. Leader of the Labour opposition Tony Blair, himself a football supporter, referred to it during his second speech to the party conference in Brighton.

'There have been good moments, like yesterday, when for the first time since I became leader, my children were impressed by something I did,' Blair said. '"Did you really meet Kevin Keegan, Dad? Did you really do 27 consecutive headers?" And wasn't it good to see Eric Cantona back in action? Let us hope this time he remembers that kicking people in the teeth is the job of the Tory government.' Nice try, but Matthew Simmons's teeth had never been touched.

Away from the opportune cultural references, there was a genuine fear that something might go awry at Old Trafford. Gordon Taylor actually appealed for Cantona to be welcomed back into the game without provocation, and he was joined by Steve Bruce in pleading for calm. Even though Cantona would have been castigated for any incident, English football itself had a duty to improve.

What was most extraordinary about that afternoon is that Cantona did not receive any physical treatment from Liverpool's players, a ceasefire respected by almost every opponent that season. At precisely the time when the media assumed Cantona would be riled and rattled, poked at with a stick to test his patience and resolve, no stick was used. Cantona barely faced any loathsome abuse from supporters during away matches, and certainly nothing to match Simmons's verbal assault. Perhaps the game – and opposition players in particular – really did appreciate that Cantona had been the fall guy.

Ferguson was certainly impressed. 'Nobody's tried anything,' he told reporters in January 1996. 'Even at Chelsea and Leeds, no problem. The fans he can handle, he expects that. But the nice surprise has been the other players. And the referees, who have treated him fairly and generally haven't tried to make a name for themselves.'

It's certainly true that the Premier League had changed during Cantona's ban. If the foreign players who made their home in English football during the early years of the 1990s had been forced to alter their game to match the style of the league, 1995 brought persuasive evidence that foreign players might have the power to change the league.

The eight months of Cantona's absence saw a comparative mass immigration of foreign players renowned not for blood and thunder but for their outstanding skill. Arsenal signed Dennis Bergkamp from Inter and Chelsea brought in the great Ruud Gullit from Sampdoria. Newcastle United recruited winger David Ginola from Paris Saint-Germain, Sheffield Wednesday signed both Regi Blinker from Feyenoord and Darko Kovačević from Red Star Belgrade, while Manchester City unearthed a new cult hero in Georgi Kinkladze, who'd been on loan from Dinamo Tbilisi at Boca Juniors.

Perhaps the most important arrival was Brazilian Juninho at Middlesbrough from São Paulo. Juninho had been heralded by Brazil coach Mário Zagallo as the brightest future star of a young national team containing Roberto Carlos, Edmundo and Ronaldo, and tracked by a number of top European clubs. His decision to sign for a promoted club from an unfashionable part of northern England was emblematic of the Premier League's new pulling power. No longer were middling Premier League clubs content to kick and rush their way to success. Supporters learned that there was a world outside of English football, and they delighted in what they saw.

It was inevitable both that Cantona's success in England paved the way for this foreign influx and that the presence of these players shaped his treatment following the ban. Referees became increasingly protective of attackers from roughhouse defending, and in doing so persuaded foreign players that the Premier League was an ideal place to call home. Cantona barely benefited from this pre-Selhurst Park, but he certainly did post-return.

If the influx of foreign players helped to smooth Cantona's return, another development threatened to hamper it. In his absence, a large number of Premier League managers had adopted a three-man central defence in a 3–5–2 formation. The concern was that the extra central defender could be used to track those forwards who, like Cantona, chose to drift deep to pick up the ball and create space in behind. Ferguson was bullish about Cantona's ability to overcome the issue – and was proved right – but other observers were far less sure.

And then there were Cantona's own issues. The suspicion was that the firebrand nature of his personality, the edge that had caused his downfall, was also integral to his success. Remove – or at least quell – that strand of Cantona's character, and you risked being left with an empty husk. Was it possible to reduce the spikiness without taking away the swagger?

The mood outside Old Trafford was one of impatient relief, as if Cantona were returning from war to the warm bosom of his loving family. Unofficial merchandise sellers sold a vast array of Cantona-related items, including T-shirts with all manner of goodwill messages. One had a caricature of Cantona reading from a book entitled *How to Be a Perfect Gent*. Another marked the date with a simple message: 'Red October'. 'Return of the magnificent 7' was a popular phrase. So too were French flags adorned with Cantona's face.

One video recording shows a dog on a lead, wearing a black T-shirt emblazoned with a tribute to Cantona. It cuts to a man wearing a beret and drinking from a can of lager; truly a fusion of cultures. Elsewhere, a man read from a homemade T-shirt on which was written a poetic ode to the King: 'He's flamboyant, he's got panache; he'll be worth £10m in cash. Cantona, Cantona. Eric was born an entertainer, he was born and bred. Born to play the game, born for Man U, born to be a red.'

As he walked out, a stadium rose to salute their hero. Cantona was last out and delayed for a fraction of a moment, as if wanting to enjoy a moment of individual recognition before the team game began. David Lacey wrote that this was 'a Mancunian version of Bastille Day', while on Sky Sports commentary Martin Tyler discussed the 'second coming'. Having served his sentence, there was no doubt that Cantona was returning as a hero, not just of Manchester United but the Premier League. Cantona's collar was turned up, naturally. Ten thousand shirts in the stands were given the same treatment.

Cantona took 67 seconds to mark his return. Steve McManaman was robbed of the ball when dribbling infield, and a pass was played to Cantona on the left wing. His left-footed cross was more hopeful than accurate, but found the onrushing Butt. If Butt's finish deserved greater acclaim than the assist, this was not the day to alter scripts. 'Cantona has made a goal for Nicky Butt,' was Tyler's screamed response.

Ferguson would be left annoyed by United's performance. Despite playing at the home of their rivals and without any away support to cheer them on, Liverpool outplayed United for extended periods of the match. They had a penalty claim turned down even before Robbie Fowler's thrashed equaliser into the roof of Schmeichel's net. Then ten minutes into the second half Fowler chipped the ball over Manchester United's goalkeeper with his weaker foot and Liverpool had the lead.

If Fowler was wrestling with Newcastle's Les Ferdinand for the honour of being the form striker in the country and worthy of leading England's line alongside Alan Shearer, Cantona was not ready to be usurped on his big day. The penalty awarded by David Elleray for a foul by Jamie Redknapp on Giggs was debatable – Redknapp had got a touch on the ball but also had his hand on Giggs's shirt – but it provided Cantona with an unlikely chance to become the hero of his own hour. If the whole thing felt scripted, sport's iconic moments so often do.

United had scored only one penalty during Cantona's eight-month absence, taken by Denis Irwin during the final home game of the previous season. Even if Irwin had been on the pitch against Liverpool, it would have taken the strength of every supporter inside Old Trafford to prise the ball from Cantona's grasp. This was his happy ending.

Cantona strode up, as casually as you might walk to the shop to buy a morning paper. He side-footed the ball into the bottom right-hand corner, as David James barely offered a dive in the opposite direction. A full half-second before the ball hit the back of the net, the stadium erupted.

In celebration, Cantona ran towards the United supporters, perhaps considering meeting with them and sharing in their joy while having his shirt pulled and hair tousled. In the end, wisely deciding that entering the crowd during his comeback game was a foolish thing to do, he climbed one of the stanchions behind the goal that helped to keep the net taut. He was truly back in pole position.

The English press, who had descended upon Old Trafford like never before, gave Cantona the full treatment. Sections in the dailies were dedicated to documenting his every touch, while there were statistical assessments of his impact on the game. The headlines were typically hyperbolic: 'Ooh Star Cantona' and 'Eric de Triomphe'.

But one person no longer wanted to focus on the returning hero. Ferguson had played the media game in the build-up to the match, but he was not prepared to feed the hype any longer. The great manager was delighted to have Cantona back and presumably equally pleased with his immediate contribution, but Ferguson's mantra was always that no individual was bigger than Manchester United. That theory has been severely tested over the preceding fortnight.

'We got off to a dream start, then we forgot we were playing a game of football,' said Ferguson after the game, visibly irked. 'The hype's over, thank goodness.'

'You know what I'm gonna do here?' he continued. 'I've finished talking about Eric Cantona. I'm happy to talk about the game. I've done enough talking about Eric Cantona. Youse are unbelievable, you people.'

Despite the outpouring of positivity, Ferguson was a brilliant pragmatist. This was the first time that United had conceded twice at home in the league since December 1994, and the first time they had dropped points at home after taking the lead since that same month. In between, a circus had come to town. It would now be forcibly asked to leave.

POSTSCRIPT

'He opened my eyes to the indispensability of practice'

One of the oddities of Cantona's return against Liverpool is that it was witnessed live by so few supporters. The demolition of the North Stand considerably reduced Old Trafford's capacity, meaning that only 34,934 were present on 1 October.

With the club's next game being away from home at York City in the League Cup and domestic football then pausing for an international break, thousands of United supporters were desperate to see Cantona back in action. And so it was that 21,502 people attended a reserve team fixture between Manchester United and Leeds United on Saturday 7 October. It is a wonderful statistical quirk that the highest attendance at a football fixture in England that day was not a first-team match.

Ferguson's pre-emptive concern was that Cantona would return to the side rusty and lacking match fitness. His performance – and contribution – against Liverpool were impressive, given his time away from competitive action, but Ferguson's suspicion was that adrenaline and sheer force of personality had carried Cantona through.

And yet Ferguson had little choice but to pick him. He had piled so many eggs into one basket, offering the Frenchman a pay rise and new contract while selling other key players, that it felt like Cantona or bust. In any case, Cantona was desperate to play.

As it turned out, the manager's worries were realised. Cantona did not play badly upon his return to the team, but neither did he illuminate the side quite as Ferguson would have liked. He picked up the occasional niggling injury, including one in the reserve team game against Leeds. In his first three months back, Cantona scored twice from open play. By then Ferguson was defending his form from media criticism. The unsurprising conclusion in some quarters was that Cantona had been becalmed.

'Yes, we've had the dip,' Ferguson admitted on 20 January. 'More than one, actually. There have been periods where his form has been off for a couple of games and he's come back quite well. So there's been an inconsistency. But that's no surprise to us. It's what we expected. And when you're judging a player there's a difference between a bad game and a flat game.'

Ferguson even conceded that the departure of Kanchelskis had hampered Cantona's form, and believed United were not always set up to get the best out of their star. But, typically, there was an insistence that the problem was temporary; Eric would be back. As so often with Ferguson, he was proved spectacularly right.

'He's been magnificent in training, just like he always has, ever since he came here,' Ferguson concluded. 'It has been difficult for him. But when he gets his consistency back, his best form will be back too.'

And how. If Ferguson and Cantona were being questioned in January, they were laughing longest and last by May. If the comeback against Liverpool gave Cantona the chance to bask once again in the adoration of the Old Trafford crowd, he vindicated Ferguson's faith with his pivotal role in helping United become the first English team to win the Double more than once.

The title race that season is generally viewed through the prism of Newcastle United's collapse, Kevin Keegan's 'love it, love it' meltdown and Ferguson proving himself to be the master of mind games. But while it is true that Newcastle's domestic form suffered an implosion (21 points dropped in their final 13 league games), Manchester United enjoyed an outstanding run of results, fuelled by the sensational performances of Cantona.

Having failed to score between 9 December and 6 January, Cantona ended his mini-drought with a late equaliser against Sunderland in the FA Cup third round. He went on to score in four of United's five FA Cup rounds en route to the final, and in nine of their final 15 league games as United dropped only five points from mid-January onwards.

So dependent on Cantona had the team become, and so capable was he at shouldering that responsibility, that no other United player but him scored a league goal between 25 February and 6 April. Seven of United's final 15 games ended 1–0; Cantona scored the winner in five of them.

By March, Ferguson was waxing lyrical about his centre-forward. 'It has been a big week for us, and we showed a few nerves among the younger players,' he said after another 1–0 win, this time against Tottenham. 'But Eric Cantona is an inspiration. I get tired of saying how magnificent he is.' Nobody cared to point out that Ferguson's last line was a blatant lie. The manager's smile said it all.

For Ferguson, the title was the only true way to guarantee credit for taking a chance on Cantona. For Cantona, the title was the only true way to repay Ferguson's faith. 'My confidence dates from the day United got me to sign up again,' he told reporters before the FA Cup final. 'I have tried to pay back Alex Ferguson in kind.'

Ferguson's ultimate gesture was to make Cantona his stand-in captain in the absence of Bruce, and it came as no surprise to his United teammates. 'We don't have to be told how important Eric is for the team, because we all know,' said Giggs. 'I don't think anyone in the dressing room thought that he wouldn't come back, but Eric is key.'

Cantona had scored in the league against Liverpool, marking his return to the team with that impromptu pole dance, but his true redemption came against them at Wembley. In becoming the first foreign national to captain a team to FA Cup final victory, Cantona rubber stamped his status as a trailblazer. And in scoring the winner in yet another 1–0 win, he lifted a dour and meandering final out of mediocrity and into immortality.

But Cantona's winner was not the most telling moment. As he walked up the 39 steps at Wembley to collect his medal and lift the famous old trophy above his head, Cantona was spat at by a Liverpool supporter. There would be no reaction this time. Cantona had suffered, coped and waited. Nothing would – nothing could – spoil his day of atonement.

Almost as significant on a personal level for Cantona was being bestowed the Football Writers' Association Player of the Year award by the industry that had been so universally scathing of his actions less than 18 months before. Cantona was the first Manchester United player to win the award since Best in 1968.

The *Guardian*'s David Lacey had touted Cantona for the award in March, but did not consider him a likely winner. 'The personal choice will lie between Steve Bruce, Dwight Yorke and Ruud Gullit,' Lacey wrote. 'But a computer, fed with the necessary calculations, might come up with another who for the last year has served his club, his supporters and his community in equal measure with neither a foot nor a word out place. Name of Eric Cantona.'

Eventually, Cantona's stellar form made Lacey's colleagues' decision for them; Cantona was impossible to ignore. An award handed out by an organisation whose own stipulations stated 'should go to the player who, by precept and example, on the field and off, shall be considered to have done most for football' was given to a player they had labelled as an *enfant terrible* the previous January. It made for quite the story arc.

Had Cantona changed? He, perhaps true to form, believed not. 'I often get asked about the change in my temperament since the incident at Crystal Palace. The truth is there hasn't been such a big change. People think I've suddenly learned to feel at ease with myself, but the fact of the matter is that I was never ill at ease in the first place.'

Conversely, Ferguson detected a notable shift in Cantona's behaviour and praised his player for that improvement. 'Since he came back into the team there have been refereeing decisions that he hasn't agreed with but he's chosen not to argue. I've seen him walk quietly away from incidents that might have drawn a different reaction before.'

The truth most likely lies somewhere in between. Cantona did not change intrinsically as a person, but his eight months away from the game did teach him the value of reining in the extremes of his personality, particularly his tendency to fight perceived injustice in such a volatile manner. On the football field, the most successful leader learns to pick his battles carefully. Some simply aren't worth fighting.

But Cantona also changed not only because he felt it necessary, but also to repay Ferguson – and therefore Manchester United – for their continued trust. There's an acceptance by him in hindsight that the decision to stay in England, largely ensured by Ferguson's covert Paris mission, was the right call. If Serie A might conceivably have been a good home, Inter probably would not have been.

Of course, Cantona did not hang around at Old Trafford long into his dotage. His was the personality type that is only prepared to live, never merely to exist. Staying a footballer deep into his 30s, as his body began to fail and the magic to erode, was never his style. As he so candidly said, 'I loved the game but I no longer had the passion to go to bed early, not to go out with my friends, not to drink, and not to do a lot of other things, the things I like in life.' That is as classically Cantona as any of his wonderful contributions on the pitch.

Ferguson did harbour some personal guilt for Cantona quitting when he did. He knew that Cantona had great hopes of European success with United, which the club would only realise in the years following his departure. For all Ferguson was vindicated in 1995/96, he later accepted that pushing the club towards signing, for example, Gabriel Batistuta, might have made the difference against Borussia Dortmund in the European Cup semi-final in 1997.

It's a view that Gary Neville agrees with. 'Failure hadn't been down to him,' he wrote in his autobiography. 'It was because we were a young, inconsistent side still exploring our potential. His departure means that he fell short of achieving his dream of conquering Europe.'

But if Cantona's retirement in 1997 caused a shockwave across English football and dismayed United's squad and manager, Ferguson was understanding. As the closest thing Cantona got to a father figure in football, deep down Ferguson knew it would end this way. Just as Nina Simone sang, stars go like the last light of the sun, all in a blaze. Cantona was not one for sliding into mediocrity.

'I don't feel let down,' said Ferguson. 'There can't be any recriminations in my heart.' Nor could there have been any among Manchester United supporters. Remorse is natural when someone special departs suddenly, but sadness can only ever give way to gratitude. Better to have loved and lost a player like Cantona than never to have watched him play at all. He was their superstar and their everyman.

Cantona was already immortal at Old Trafford – before the kung-fu kick, the ban, the return and the double. When he left, his legacy was partly the memories of turned-up collars and endlessly rewound and replayed goals on video tapes, but mostly the generation of young players he inspired to become Manchester United's next great team.

It is left to Ferguson to summarise his greatest player better perhaps than any author can: 'Many people have justifiably acclaimed Cantona as a catalyst who had a crucial impact on our success while he was with the club, but nothing he did in matches meant more than the way he opened my eyes to the indispensability of practice. Practice makes players.' The United manager had his mantra for the club's new era.

BIBLIOGRAPHY

Anon. 'Cantona fan is jailed for attacking lawyer',
   Independent website, 3 May 1996

Anon. *Cantona: Return of the King – A Sky Sports Originals
   Story*, Sky Sports, 4 October 2015

Anon. 'Cantona: The madness of the King', *The42.ie*,
   25 May 2016

Auclair, Philippe. *Cantona: The Rebel Who Would Be King*,
   London: Macmillan, 2009

Bateman, Cynthia. 'A kick too far for Cantona?', *Guardian*,
   13 February 1995

Bierley, Stephen. 'The shame of Cantona', *Guardian*,
   27 January 1995

Boggan, Steve. 'Jail term may make Cantona quit UK',
   Independent website, 24 March 1995

Burnton, Simon. 'Eric Cantona's kung-fu kick 20 years on
   – the night that changed football forever', *Guardian*
   website, 23 January 2015

Cantona, Eric. *Cantona: My Story*, London: Headline, 1994

Coman, Julian. 'The King and I: meeting Eric Cantona',
   Guardian website, 25 March 2012

Edwards, Martin. *Red Glory: Manchester United and Me*,
   London: Michael O'Mara, 2017

Fawbert, Dave. 'How Eric Cantona's kung-fu kick changed my life', *Shortlist*, 24 January 2018

Ferguson, Alex. *A Year in the Life: The Manager's Diary*, London: Virgin Publishing, 1995

Ferguson, Alex. *A Will to Win: The Manager's Diary*, London: André Deutsch, 1997

Ferguson, Alex. *Managing My Life*, London: Hodder & Stoughton, 1999

Ferguson, Alex. *Leading*, London: Hodder & Stoughton, 2016

Fowler, Robbie. *My Autobiography*, London: Pan Macmillan, 2005

Fynn, Alex and Cantona, Eric. *Cantona on Cantona: Reflections of a Sporting Legend*, London: André Deutsch, 1996

Gamboa, Inaki. 'Cantona: I should have kicked that Crystal Palace fan harder', *Marca* website, 23 February 2017

Hackett, Robin and Atkin, Nick. 'When Manchester United's Eric Cantona attacked a fan in 1995', ESPN website, 25 January 2015

Hibbs, Ben and Marshall, Adam. *Red Leaders: The Official Story of Manchester United's Captains*, London: Simon & Schuster, 2014

Hughes, Mark. *Hughesie!: The Story of Mark Hughes*, London: Mainstream, 1994

Lacey, David. 'Cantona hits fan, faces lengthy ban', *Guardian*, 26 January 1995

Lacey, David. 'Cantona turns the screw', *Guardian*,
5 March 1996

Lacey, David. 'This year Cantona earns stamp of approval',
Guardian, 30 March 1996

Film4, *Looking for Eric* DVD, 2009

Luckhurst, Samuel. 'Manchester United 2–2 Liverpool: Eric
Cantona's 1995 comeback', *Manchester Evening News*
website, 1 October 2015

Marshall, Ian. *Class of 92*, London: Simon & Schuster,
2012

Mathieson, Stuart. 'Pallister: Fergie never lost it with
Cantona, not even at Palace!', *Manchester Evening News*
website, 21 January 1995

Miller, Nick. 'Quote unquote: Cantona and his seagulls',
Football365, 13 October 2016

Mullin, John. 'Cantona banned for the season', *Guardian*,
28 January 1995

Mullin, John. 'Fish-quoter Cantona clucks the cells',
Guardian, 1 April 1995

Neville, Gary. *Red: My Autobiography*, London: Bantam
Press, 2011

Ridley, Ian. *Cantona: The Red and the Black*, London:
Gollancz, 1995

Smyth, Rob. 'Manchester United 2 Liverpool 2', *The
Blizzard*, 1 September 2015

Søren, Frank. *Standing on the Shoulders of Giants: A
Cultural Analysis of Manchester United*, London:
Bloomsbury, 2008

Taylor, Daniel. *This Is the One – Sir Alex Ferguson: The Uncut Story of a Football Genius*, London: Aurum Press, 2007

Tomas, Jason. 'Cantona "not for sale" insists Ferguson', *Observer*, 26 February 1995

Tulett, Darren. 'The assailant', *Guardian* website, 31 October 2004

Williams, Richard. 'A martyr to his own myth', *Independent* website, 29 January 1995

Williams, Richard. 'Cantona ready to blossom again: Ferguson sees the end of a "flat spell" in sight', *Guardian*, 20 January 1996